Snappy lemon
1/4 soy sauce
2 T. wine
T. lemon

8-10 min.

Butter Bonbons
powdered sugar
soft butter
peanut butter
chopped walnuts (optional)
vanilla
pkg. milk choc chips
wax strip   2 T. oil
over a well + form into

German Choc. Cake + Frosting
white cake mix
inst. choc pudding
eggs
milk

German
cake mix + 1/2 sour cream

Hot.
3 lb cheese   cheddar, sharp
1 litre wine - 2/3 of wine in pot
clove garlic, rub garlic
almost boil, not boil

Ruthiebelle's Baked Stuffed Clams

4 lbs. minced clams   1 can (15 oz) italian season br crumbs
1 1/2 " bacon
2 1/2 " onions   salt, pepper, accent
Grind each above   garlic powder, Parmesan cheese
approx. 20 min. mix   separately + cook (simmer)
garlic powder, + br crumbs + juice, drained
with clam juice, + cheese, to taste, pepper
clam shells. Bake at 350° to
makes   my own recipe

Sue Fields 3/0:

Stuffed Mushrooms
seasoned bread crumbs
margerine
chopped olives
bacon bits (real)
lg. mushrooms
Pull off mushroom stems + chop fine. saute in
margerine. Add seasoned bread crumbs,
olives, bacon, + some reserved bacon dripping
may need to add additional water - to moisten
mixture. Stuff in mushroom caps. Bake at
350 x 20 min til hot + browned.

of foil on shallow roasting pan.
smoke over + under meat (3 1/2 oz bottle).
6 hrs @ 250°
liquid smoke
(optional)
baste with sauce every 15 min during last hour.

simmer:
1 tsp oregano   use extra sauce
1 tsp marjoram   on baked potatoes
1 tsp sweet basil   slice meat thinly
1 tsp pepper   after it sits
                     for 15 minutes

sauce
sugar
oil

4 c. brown sugar
1 can corned beef
1 T. vinegar

Brown hamburger. Add rest of ingredients
Simmer 1 hr. Serve on hamburger buns.

CK. ...
1½ lbs. ck. breasts 2 or 3
1 pk. brocoll frozen cooked (slightly c
1 can cr. of ck. soup   sm. pieces
sauce { ½ c. mayo
       ½ t. Lem. juice
       ½ t. curry powder

cheese on top 1-1½ c.
½ c. bread crumbs } mixed
1 T butter

25 min. – 350°

barely grease casserole
place cook't Froz. Broc
ck. on top of Broc – par boil – skin off
small pieces (eggs)

sift ...
Beat eggs & ...
grad add sugar ...
on juice – fold in ...
sprinkle nuts on top
15 min. ... turn
... led with ...
... roll ...

Choc. Chip Cookies   350°

1 C shortening
2 c sugar   } cream
1 c Br. "
2 t. vanilla

3 eggs
2 t. salt
2 t. soda
3 C flour   2½   1 c oat
6 – 12 oz choc. chips

... 2 ye...
2 eggs
5-6 cups 1...

... milk with shortening, sugar, sa...
... es in lukewarm water. When milk
... en eggs. Add flour to make a s...
... ice. Roll out and spread doug...
... (white or brown) add raisins o...
... cinnamon. Roll up like jelly ro...
... ch thick. Pr... greased pan ...
... bled in bu... about 15...

Cream Pie (mother's)

¼ c. corn starch   Mix cornstarch, ⅔ c sugar & salt
⅔ c. sugar   and add milk. cook in
¼ tsp. salt   dbl boiler til thick, about 10
2 c. milk scalded   min. stirring constantly.
3 slightly beaten yolks Slowly add hot mixture to
2 tbs. butter   egg yolks, stir into re...
½ tsp. vanilla extract hot mixture ...
1 9 in. baked pie shell
3 stiff beaten
6 t ...

Serves 6
great for brunch

Bacon & Egg Bake

8 bacon slices
2 med. onions, sliced
1 can. cr. of Mush soup
¼ c. milk
5 hard cooked eggs, sliced
2 c. (8 oz) shredded cheese
salt & pepper, dash
Eng. muffins, split-toasted

Heat oven to 350°. Fry Bacon until crisp,
remove from skillet. Drain fat reserving 2 T.
Saute onion ...   Stir in soup,
milk, eggs, chee...

Minestrone Soup

Dice 5 slices of bacon (½ lb)
or onion sliced (2)
2 cloves garlic minced
1 jar spaghetti sauce (15 oz)
6 C. water   5 c.
2 beef bouillan cubes
1½ c. each celery & carrots, sliced

BBQUED B
5-8 lbs beef br...
Put meat in large
Pour ½ bottle of
Seal foil tightly.
After 3 hours ...
Uncover during last
Cut off excess fat the

SAUCE:
Mix over medium hea...
½ stick butter
1 cup brown sugar
1 heaping Tbs. d...
... cup ...
excellent!
Westchester land cook'd...

1 lg. zucchini
1 16 oz. kidney beans
½ c. macaroni – tiny sh...
1 T. parsley
Thinly sliced Turkey kilbasa

... Sundried -
Pasta

... minced garlic in olive oil
... saute
... Broc. cook down s...
1 C. Ck. Broth... cook down ...
... little Sundried tomatos
... pasta 2 ...

Life At Our Table

RECIPES FOR GATHERING AND CONNECTING

Life At Our Table

RECIPES FOR GATHERING AND CONNECTING

The Moore Family

p. 256 CREDIT LINE: Excerpt(s) from 40 YEARS OF CHEZ PANISSE: THE POWER OF GATHERING
by Alice Waters, copyright © 2011 by Alice Waters. Used by permission of Clarkson Potter Publishers, an
imprint of the Crown Publishing Group, a division of Penguin Random House LLC. All rights reserved.

ISBN: 979-8-9882362-4-5
Library of Congress Control Number: 2024924022

Book Cover and Interior Designer: Brooke Williams
Book Cover and Interior Photographer: Alice Nelson
Food Stylist: Suzy Eaton
Food Stylist Assistant: Danni Powell
Freelance Writer/Editor: Camille Smith
Recipe Editor: Deri Reed
Copyeditor: Catherine Pavia
Indexer: Rachel Lyon

Printed in China
10 9 8 7 6 5 4 3 2 1
First Edition: April 2025

Jumelle Press
3350 S. 2940 E. #9690
Salt Lake City, UT 84109
www.jumellepress.com
@jumellepress

Dedicated to everyone who has
or will join us and connect at our table

Life At Our Table

RECIPES FOR GATHERING AND CONNECTING

To my first crowded table: Mom, Dad, Tiff, Dani, and David,

This book is a memoir of our family, told through food, our love language for over 50 years. Our childhood beneath Mt. Diablo in Walnut Creek, California was idyllic. We grew up washing Mom and Dad's cars on Saturdays and snapping photos with disposable cameras by the pool. We celebrated each day with a meal— and if we were lucky, fork fights for the last bits of chocolate molten cake. Although years have passed and we "grow'd up" (as one of my twins would say), our culture of gathering, cooking, and feeding is alive and evolving.

To the world's best siblings: Tiffany, so full of life, you have taken Los Angeles by storm, embracing the journeys of entrepreneurship and motherhood with such wisdom and grace. Danielle, the most stylish Moore, you bring people together and build community in your home, a sanctuary where our family culture and values shine. David, the epitome of perseverance, you are the most thoughtful of us, never shying away from hard conversations and always building strong bonds.

Mom and Dad, you showed us that to be a Moore is to gather and feed, because if we didn't step up to host, who would? From weeknight dinners to neighborhood barbecues to epic bashes, you always made room for one more (or another 10) at our table. In all areas of life, you led by example. By watching you exercise, we learned to take care of ourselves first. By watching you give of yourselves, we saw the value of serving others. By watching you learn, we understood the importance of growth. By watching your faith in action, we experienced the blessings of making Jesus a priority.

In writing this book, we gathered with one another and compiled our favorite recipes from throughout the years. The memories and stories connected to each recipe are what I cherish most.

Kristin

Take a Seat at Our Table

Decked out in matching OshKosh outfits and large perms (for the Moore girls!), we once went door-to-door selling tickets for a neighborhood talent show. Family and friends squeezed into our home wherever there was room between the leotards, scooters, and dance shoes blanketing the floor. Behind the guests was a smorgasbord of our family's favorite foods. The talent wasn't spectacular, but the feeling in the room was magical!

This was the home we grew up in, one that invited people to feel at ease and eat good food. As a Moore family saying goes, "It's either a good time or a good story, and if you're lucky...it's both!" Our parents' open-door, open-heart policy meant our home was always full of good times and good stories. Whether it was talent shows, movie nights, or backyard barbecues, we gathered old friends and new for anything and everything. We still do!

Connection has always been important to our family, and we do it best at a food-filled table! It's how we show our love. Whether in spotless dining rooms, encircling second-hand grills, or even sitting criss-cross applesauce on the floor, we show people that they matter by feeding them—body and soul. Connection is the underlying thread through decades of cooking, hosting, and loving.

Our mom, Laurie Gunter Moore, is an amazing cook and gatherer, but she didn't grow up that way. Her mom, our Grandma Dot, wasn't much of a cook (her words, not ours!). Mom only began to cook after she and our dad, Doug, moved to Rhode Island as newlyweds. There, Mom met Christine Stevenson, a lifelong friend who opened her recipe box to Mom and shared the joys of cooking. Before long, Mom adopted the Thomas Keller approach in the kitchen: first, follow a recipe exactly; second, rewrite it; and third, never look at it again!

Dad—as good at barbecuing as he is at washing dishes—always shared the fun and hard work of hosting. On a warm California day, you'd find him at the grill, surrounded by kids, tending ribs, flank steak, or filets as he imparted advice about boyfriends, careers, and the stock market. Together, our parents showed us what it means to connect with others. Their favorite way to do this was around the table, sharing stories over the backdrop of clinking forks and messy mouths.

Our parents never formally taught us to cook: we learned this art through observing and participating. We understand flavors by feel, not measurements. Our tables have become blank canvases, our kitchens have become our work stations, and every day our food is our masterpiece—even if it is doctored mac 'n cheese.

Now, with our own families, we replicate this love of gathering, connecting, and showing up. We each have hosted through the years, squeezing loved ones into tiny apartments or large homes. Neither space nor budget ever stopped a Moore from throwing open the door and inviting people for no other reason than just wanting them to be fed and nourished from our table.

As we considered writing this book, we wanted it to be about something more than just recipes. Our family always showed up for others—in the community, in church, with family, and for each other. The Scottsdale swim team needed a director? Dad was their man. The Junior League needed a volunteer? Mom was first in line! Bringing meals for the sick, moving a neighbor, visiting the elderly? It's just what they did. They showed up day after day, year after year, always finding more bandwidth and always finding more space in their huge hearts. As the saying goes, "You can pretend to care, but you can't pretend to show up."

Our lives haven't been all parties and backyard barbecues. As with many families, ours has been touched by the effects of addiction—uncles, cousins, grandparents, and even our brother, David. We don't shy away from this issue. David's message is one to shout from the rooftops: Connection is the opposite of addiction. Connection is prevention! The greatest way to support someone through addiction and substance abuse is to love and connect with them. That starts with showing up.

We are excited that proceeds from the sale of this cookbook will go toward substance abuse education and prevention. Whether or not you or your family have been touched by addiction, we hope our message brings you closer to those you care about.

Writing this cookbook was challenging because our recipes are in our heads! We take full creative license in our kitchens, so measurements always change. However,

NEITHER SPACE NOR BUDGET EVER STOPPED
A MOORE FROM THROWING OPEN THE DOOR
AND INVITING PEOPLE FOR NO OTHER
REASON THAN JUST WANTING THEM TO
BE FED AND NOURISHED FROM OUR TABLE.

to pass down these recipes to our own kids, we knew it was time to figure out exactly how much of "this and that" we actually use! After much time in the kitchen (and plenty of back and forth among siblings), you can rest assured you're getting the Moore family recipes at their best—complete with measurements, easy-to-follow instructions, and so much love. That said, we aren't perfectionists. So if a recipe doesn't quite work out, or seems to be missing a step, feel free to improve upon it and make it your own!

In this cookbook, we share our favorite breakfasts (including our famous **Egg, Ham, and Spinach en Croute, see page 33**, and always-asked-for **Cinnamon French Toast Bake, see page 34**); You'll find finger-friendly appetizers, our Mom's famous salads (I'm looking at you **Apple Pecan Salad, see page 87!**), Traeger favorites on repeat—did someone say **Million Dollar Bacon**?! **(see page 121)**, the best sides and throwbacks to put the comfort in comfort food, and some hassle-free desserts to end your meal on a sweet note.

Whether you are making food for your little family or creating a beautiful spread for a large gathering, you'll find recipes here that have been tested, talked about, and loved for years and years—from our table to yours.

So pick a recipe and invite someone over! Anything is worth celebrating. Take it from the Moores who've long believed that a small gathering of siblings and friends in swimsuits or leotards is a perfect reason to break out the famous bean dip (see page 71). ***Parties? Yes, please! And the "Moore," the merrier!***

Our Crowded Table

When we were growing up, our table was a warm, inclusive place to connect. The literal table was always clean, set immaculately, and included a salad and vegetable at every meal. On school nights, we worked through algebra homework and English essays at the table. If we needed help, we scratched Dad's bald head, knowing that the longer the massage, the more help we would get!

After dinner, the whole family pitched in to clean to perfection. No one wanted dustbuster duty, so whoever was "closest to the floor" was relegated to the task, and that depended on who missed dinner for dance class or sports practice. Usually, we had a small but yummy dessert of sugary cereal, or we stole some of Dad's coffee ice cream and poured some "cracklin" Nestle chocolate sauce on top as we turned on Nick at Nite.

Now in 2025, perfectly set weeknight tables, "real" dishes, and sparkling floors seem to be a thing of the past. The kids are busy and schedules are hectic (or so we tell ourselves). Family dinner nowadays is a little bit more casual than it was growing up. We rely too heavily on disposable plates and take-out for dinner and could use the dustbuster a little bit more—except for Dani, who has followed Mom's "neatnik" personality. Although the table may look and feel a little different, we have each adopted the best parts of the Moore family crowded table in our own homes and have made them uniquely ours.

Kristin is a party-planning machine. From throwing bashes all by herself to hiring them out, she loves throwing her own birthday parties and hosting community events. Tiffany is the scrappiest party planner. She is a pro at cooking and hosting for any size group, in any space, and never lets last-minute changes throw off her game. Danielle loves the details and planning that go into a big bash, which is why hers are always so successful. Then there's David, who has followed in Dad's footsteps, grilling all the good stuff for his family.

Let's be honest—crowded tables are way more fun than empty ones! That's why none of us ever waited until we had the big home, "enough" moncy, or fancy napkins to begin inviting others into our spaces. We threw Christmas parties in tiny Sugar House bungalows, birthday parties in San Francisco studio apartments, and weekend get-togethers in Los Angeles student housing. We knew that gathering was not about perfect food or over-the-top floral arrangements. In truth, it was about creating a space for others to leave their day at the door, enjoy the gifts of rest and reprieve, and feel a sense of belonging.

WHY OUR PARENTS GATHERED

Our Dad comes from a family that has been gathering others for years and years. Our grandma, Ruth Moore, grew up without much. Her mom, Nellie McCory, started taking people into her home in return for meager rent. A dozen or more guests would stay at any given time, and Nellie would cook for them. Grandma Ruth grew up in this nursing home of sorts. Her son—our dad—remembers "fantastic eating" when the family gathered. Grandma Ruth continued her mom's legacy of inviting people in and feeding them.

Once Grandma Ruth passed, our parents took up the banner of hosting. It started in their little three-story walk-up apartment in Rhode Island. After making homemade Concord grape juice from their landlady's grape farm, they served a large pitcher to some guests from their church community. Not realizing that grape juice is typically diluted with water, their pure grape juice had all their guests cracking up at each other's bright purple Smurf mouths! Moments like these are the building blocks for great relationships with new friends.

We could tell story after story of these memorable moments, but the point is that if you gather and feed people, these moments are guaranteed! That's the legacy our grandparents began and our parents passed on. And it's the legacy us Moore kids carry on, too. When we welcome people into our homes and feed them, we provide two of the most basic human needs: food and shelter. We also show guests that there is space for them in our lives—a place where they matter.

WHY WE GATHER TODAY

Seeing our parents host over the years, we realized a gathering isn't about the size of the space or the fanciness of the food you serve. It's all about the people. Our parents didn't host to impress guests with their house or even with the food—they just wanted to get people together. Deep down, we all want a place to go, a place to feel a part of something. People are just grateful to have somewhere they are wanted—where people will invite them, accept them, and feed their souls. We've adopted that "why" and now each of us loves the moments when new friends show up with kids, swim goggles, and big appetites in tow, all wanting to partake of that special feeling: community. Gathering around the table is just an easy (and delicious!) way to do it.

WHEN YOU HAVE MORE THAN YOU NEED, BUILD A LONGER TABLE NOT A HIGHER FENCE.

When we break down fences, invite people into our homes, and to join us around our tables, we honor each person's value in this world.

IMPORTANT COMPONENTS FOR GATHERING

For us, the most important components for gathering are connection, ambience, and food! When each element is purposeful, life-changing moments and life-enriching connections with new friends are made. Creating the right ambience doesn't require elaborate decorations or decorations at all, for that matter. It's all about creating a space for people to feel welcome. Kristin experienced the humblest of welcomes when she sat on a turquoise carpet with new Nepalese friends who served up their family recipes of fragrant rice and juicy chicken while sharing how their grandparents immigrated to Utah with just $5 to their name. Danielle and her husband, Parin, create this connection through an open-door culture with family and friends. They have friends over almost every weekend. Parin fires up the Traeger, and that's when the magic happens—when people connect over good food and good company. Living in Los Angeles, Tiffany has surrounded herself with so many people from different walks of life by sharing her warm living space with others as they enjoy soul-filling food together. Food has always been a social time in our family because we treat it as an event instead of just a meal. Getting a small group gathered in your home, your backyard, or at a park is a great way to make meaningful connections.

THE MAGIC AND MEMORIES ARE IN THE MESS— AND SO IS THE LOVE AND CHAOS AND FUN!

HOW CAN YOU CREATE YOUR OWN "CROWDED TABLE"?

Whether you have a small space for hosting or a yard fit for large barbecues, our hope is that you reach out to old friends and new friends, throw open your doors, and break out the fine china (read: paper plates!). We hope you embrace having your couch cushions scattered in fort-making and pillow fights, that you raid your fridge and lay out a buffet (or serve pizza with chips and dip. It's all the same in the end). We hope your home is filled with dirty dishes, boisterous laughter, and shared stories, and that your floors are dirtied with the crumbs of loved ones, hurt ones, broken ones, and renewed ones. The magic and memories are in the mess—and so is the love and chaos and fun! This mentality has blessed our entire family and we know it will bless yours. You have "Moore" fun and you make "Moore" friends when "Moore" are invited!

Must-Have Supplies

Whether we are throwing together a dish for a spontaneous ladies' lunch or kids' hangout or prepping for a holiday party weeks in advance, having a regularly stocked kitchen with favorites stashed in the fridge, freezer, and pantry is our secret to planning in a pinch.

We keep things simple when it comes to supplies we use for cooking and serving (other than perhaps a slight obsession with platters—we blame you, Mom!). We always use our fine Chinet (you know, paper plates, plastic cutlery) and invest in the best items for keeping food warm while serving (we love a good disposable aluminum roasting pan!).

Here's a cheat sheet of what we always have on hand in our homes so we are ready for anything!

THE STAPLES

PROTEIN

eggs (hard boiled and fresh), sliced turkey meat, lean ground chicken or turkey, rotisserie chicken (can freeze to thaw when needed), prosciutto, shredded pork, and bacon pieces. Protein freezer staples for weeknight dinners: chicken breast, chicken thigh, pork tenderloin, and salmon.

DAIRY

almond milk, vanilla Greek yogurt, cottage cheese, cheddar cheese, goat cheese, feta cheese, Parmesan, blue cheese crumbles, Monterey Jack cheese, Swiss cheese, burrata balls. Most of these can easily be kept in the freezer.

FRUIT

strawberries, bananas, blueberries, raspberries, small apples, cuties, oranges, nectarines, limes

VEGGIES

mini peppers, onions (whole or pre-chopped), spinach, large bag of power greens from Costco (kept in freezer), arugula, frozen hash browns, avocados, bagged broccoli, green beans, pre-chopped squash, tomatoes, sweet potatoes, red new potatoes, carrots (shredded or matchstick), mushrooms, bell peppers

BREAKFAST BASICS

See Chapter 1

MIX-INS/TOPPINGS
ground flaxseed, mini chocolate chips, raisins, chia seeds, slivered almonds, honey, protein powder

BAKING SUPPLIES
cinnamon, baking soda/baking powder, vanilla extract, brown sugar, butter (in the freezer)

NUT BUTTERS
peanut butter, almond butter

BREADS
puff pastry, cinnamon bread, sourdough bread, wheat sandwich bread

ROLLED OATS/STEEL CUT OATS

NECESSITIES TO BUILD THE PERFECT APPETIZER

See Chapter 2

CRACKERS/CHIPS
tortilla chips, crostini crackers, pita chips, baguette (can store in the freezer until ready to use), almond thins

CANNED GOODS
black beans, chili, corn, green chilies, black olives, garlic, chopped tomatoes

SAUCES
salsa/pico de gallo, soy sauce, toasted sesame oil, pesto, olive oil, BBQ sauce

INGREDIENTS FOR DIPS
sour cream, Greek yogurt, hummus, honey, fresh herbs

TOPPINGS
bacon pieces (we love to shop for this at the salad bar and freeze any extra), toasted pine nuts, scallions, cilantro, flat-leaf parsley, prosciutto, dates

STARCHES
frozen brown rice (we get the kind from Trader Joes, freeze it, then thaw as needed), small potatoes

MOST-USED INGREDIENTS FOR SALADS

See Chapter 3

LEAFY GREENS
romaine lettuce/red leaf lettuce, arugula, spinach, iceberg, bagged cabbage, butter lettuce

TOASTED NUTS
almonds, pecans, pistachios, etc. (toast nuts in a large batch ahead of time and store in the freezer to grab when needed)

DRIED FRUIT
dates, cherries, cranberries, golden raisins, currants

FRESH FRUIT
mangoes, watermelon, persimmons, pomegranate seeds, and peaches

VEGETABLES
purple onions, Brussels sprouts, corn (we prefer frozen over canned)

HOMEMADE SALAD DRESSINGS
(SEE PAGE 102)
olive oil, balsamic vinegar, red wine vinegar, minced garlic, finely diced onions, salt and pepper

MAKE YOUR TRAEGER FAVORITES

See Chapter 4

PROTEIN
flank steak, baby back pork ribs, lobster tails, thick-cut bacon, filet mignon, and steaks

RUBS
Traeger pork & poultry rub, Traeger chicken rub, Trager coffee rub

SAUCES
Traeger 'Que BBQ sauce, Traeger Sugar Lips glaze, soyaki/teriyaki sauce, Sriracha

MARINADE ADDITIONS
yellow mustard, apple juice, brown sugar, honey, maple syrup, apricot jam, scallions, sliced lemons/oranges

FRESH HERBS
rosemary and thyme sprigs, cilantro, fresh parsley

SPICES
frozen garlic cubes from Trader Joes, oregano, cumin, cayenne pepper, flavored salts, onion salt, garlic powder, salt & pepper (for seasoning rubs or marinades)

See Chapter 5

SPICES
rosemary, nutmeg, cayenne pepper, cumin, curry powder, paprika, garlic powder, salt & pepper

SAUCES
Worcestershire sauce, soy sauce, lime juice, apple cider vinegar

FAVORITE MARINADE
(see page 162)
olive oil, balsamic glaze, minced garlic, salt & pepper

KITCHEN AND SERVING SUPPLIES

Platters, platters, platters!

Big wooden boards

Water dispenser

Ice canister

Large cookie sheets

Meat thermometer (Meater or Thermapen)

Staub or enameled cast-iron cookware

Traeger grill and Flatrock griddle

Baking dishes (glass 9x13-inch pans)

Sauté pans

Grilling tools

Wipeable placemats

Disposable aluminum roasting pans

Paper/plastic goods

Light wood pellets like apple, cherry, pecan (for Traeger)

CHAPTER 1

Morning Huddle

From making pancakes on Sundays after church growing up, to blending protein shakes on weekdays before school, our family has always valued the importance of a healthy or delicious breakfast! When we have the luxury of a slow morning, we love spending extra family time in the kitchen. With everyone contributing—cutting strawberries, cracking eggs, and stirring batter—indulgent breakfasts have become our favorite way to spend quality time together!

As our family has expanded, so has our list of favorites! In fact, it was nearly impossible to trim this list down to those we have included. Some recipes, like our **Cinnamon French Toast Bake (see page 34)**, have been crowd-pleasers for years and can feed the masses. Others, like our California citrus-inspired **Lemon Curd Chia Seed Pudding (see page 40)**, is a more recent favorite, and is perfect to keep in the fridge for grab-and-go.

As we have traveled to different parts of the world and invited people from other cultures into our homes, we have incorporated new recipes into our repertoire. On a trip to Israel, Kristin was introduced to **Shakshuka**, a Mediterranean tomato and egg dish common in North Africa and the Middle East. Once home, she developed her own variation **(see page 44)**. It is not only the flavors we crave after trying something new, but also the transformative effect food has—in this case the aroma of spices and sizzle of the cast-iron skillet—which take us back to a specific moment in time, reminding us of places we've been and people we've come to love.

These recipes represent the best of the best, with something for everyone. It wouldn't be Christmas morning without Mom's famous **Egg, Ham, and Spinach en Croute (see page 33)**, and it wouldn't be a Moore freezer without a container of homemade **Peanut Butter Protein Poppers (see page 39)**. As our answer for an easy meal is often "breakfast for dinner," we encourage you to make any of these recipes any time!

Creamy Overnight Oats

With six children, Kristin has found creamy overnight oats to be the ideal make-ahead option for busy mornings. They are the perfect blank canvas for your family to add their favorite mix-ins and flavor combinations: peanut butter and maple syrup, cinnamon and chopped apples, or berries. We also sometimes top them with our homemade **Mix & Match Crunchy Granola (see page 49)**. We've even caught someone adding their overnight oats into a heaping bowl full of Greek yogurt. Get creative with your favorite mix-ins. You really can't go wrong! Use Dannon Light + Fit yogurt for sweeter oats.

SERVES 8

4 cups old-fashioned oats
5 cups almond or coconut milk
2 cups vanilla Greek yogurt
¼ cup chia seeds
2 tablespoons maple syrup
1 teaspoon vanilla extract
Pinch of salt

Favorite toppings
   apple, banana, peaches, blueberries, dried fruit; cinnamon, peanut butter, brown sugar, granola

Mix the oats, milk, yogurt, chia seeds, maple syrup, vanilla, and salt together in a bowl. Cover and refrigerate overnight. When you are ready to serve, remove from the fridge and add your toppings! Store any leftovers in an airtight container for up to a week.

tip There are many ways to serve this crowd-pleasing dish: You can layer toppings and oatmeal in a mason jar and serve for brunch. Lay out toppings on the counter and let your kids make their own parfaits. Or serve in a big casserole dish with toppings on the side for a crowd.

Egg, Ham, and Spinach en Croute

Laurie clipped this recipe from *The Contra Costa Times* and has been making her version ever since! Not a Christmas morning has gone by without this delicious en croute. We've tried it with more cheese, less spinach, sausage or bacon instead of ham...it all works!

SERVES 8

2 large eggs

1 **tablespoon** yellow mustard

2 **teaspoons** lemon juice

1 **package (10-ounces)** chopped frozen spinach, thawed and well-drained

4 hard-boiled eggs, peeled and chopped

1 **cup** chopped ham

1 **cup** shredded Swiss cheese

1 **sheet** Pepperidge Farm frozen puff pastry, thawed overnight in the refrigerator

1 Preheat the oven to 425°F. Lightly grease an 11x17-inch baking sheet.

2 In a large bowl, beat the eggs well, then measure out 2 tablespoons and set aside in a small bowl. Stir the mustard and lemon juice into the remaining eggs in the large bowl. Stir in the spinach, hard-boiled eggs, ham, and Swiss cheese until well combined.

4 Gently unfold the puff pastry and spread it over the baking sheet, pressing down and rolling until it covers the sheet. It will be thin. Place the filling in a horizontal line across the center of the puff pastry, stopping a half inch from the end on both sides.

5 Fold the bottom third of the puff pastry up over the mixture, then fold the top third of the puff pastry down over that. Very gently massage the en croute to spread the mixture evenly inside the pastry.

6 Brush the top and sides of the pastry with the remaining beaten eggs. Cut five shallow diagonal slashes on top. Bake for about 20 minutes, until golden brown. Remove from oven and let sit for at least 10 minutes before serving. Enjoy!

Cinnamon French Toast Bake

As children, we attended three hours of church every Sunday. Afterward, we would gather in the kitchen, ravenous, and our parents would serve us French toast as fast as they could! Carrying our love of French toast into adulthood, Kristin discovered a more efficient way to serve this ultimate comfort food when she baked a loaf of Great Harvest Cinnamon Bread in the egg and cream sauce! If you're looking for a simple breakfast recipe that can feed an army at once—and make them incredibly happy and satisfied—then this French Toast Bake is for you! Every time we make this sugary cinnamon delight, people always come back for seconds...or thirds!

SERVES 12

1 loaf cinnamon bread, challah bread, or good white bread, torn into rough 1-inch pieces
10 large eggs
4 cups whole milk or vanilla almond milk (see Tip)

¾ cup packed brown sugar
2 teaspoons cinnamon
2 teaspoons vanilla extract
Dash of salt

1   Spray a 9x13-inch casserole dish liberally with cooking spray and add the bread pieces.

2   In a mixing bowl, beat the eggs and milk. Add the brown sugar, cinnamon, vanilla, and salt and mix thoroughly. Pour the egg mixture over the bread pieces, making sure all bread is covered with liquid and push the bread down to soak all the pieces. Cover with plastic wrap and refrigerate overnight or up to 24 hours.

3   When ready to eat, preheat the oven to 350°F. Remove the plastic wrap. Bake the casserole for 30 minutes and then loosely cover it with aluminum foil and bake another 30 minutes, or until the French toast is set and golden brown You can stick a fork in and pull out some of the middle pieces to make sure it is cooked through. Serve with berries and your favorite syrup.

tip   Depending on how rich you want your casserole, you could use 2% milk or half-and-half instead of milk. Make this with torn croissants for over-the-top deliciousness. 🥄

Kitchen Sink Breakfast Hash

This should actually be called "Everything but the Kitchen Sink Hash." Some of our most-used family recipes were created out of a desire to not let food go to waste, while also not wanting to eat the same food twice! Kristin's hash is no exception. We love making crispy and comforting hash for breakfast, lunch, or dinner, but especially on Sundays when everyone seems to walk in the door starving! Since we usually have leftover meat and roasted veggies, we pull whatever we have out of the fridge, then add potatoes, bell peppers, onions, and top with eggs for a hearty breakfast!

SERVES 10–12

3 tablespoons extra-virgin olive oil
1 yellow onion, diced
1 bell pepper, diced
1 clove garlic, minced
3 cups frozen hash browns or diced
  potatoes, sautéed to warm through
2 cups shredded cooked brisket, chicken,
  or your favorite leftover protein

2 cups leftover cooked vegetables—our
  favorites are squash, Brussels sprouts,
  broccoli, and zucchini
8 large eggs
Salt & ground black pepper
Optional toppings
  hot sauce, avocado, salsa, pico de gallo,
  sour cream

1 Heat the oil in a large cast-iron skillet or sauté pan over medium heat. Add the onion and peppers and sauté until translucent, about 8 to 10 minutes. Add the garlic and cook for 3 more minutes. Add the potatoes and cook, stirring, until browned.

2 Add the meat and veggies and heat until warmed through. One by one, crack each egg on top of the hash. Cover the pan and cook over low heat until the egg whites are solid, about 6 to 8 minutes or to your desired doneness. Season with salt and pepper, top with preferred toppings, and serve.

Peanut Butter Protein Poppers

Discussing recipes is one of the many ways Kristin, Tiffany, and Danielle stay connected, despite living far apart. Kristin shared this protein popper recipe years ago and we have all been making them ever since—even our kids like them! These protein-packed poppers are tried and tested, and we always have a batch of these on hand in the freezer. They are an easy and delicious way to get in a nutritious breakfast while rushing out the door, a perfect protein treat for a post-workout or soccer-practice energy boost, and a great substitute for dessert. Our family is obsessed!

MAKES 24

3 **cups** creamy nut butter (not natural or chunky)

2 **cups** old-fashioned oats

2 **cups** steel-cut oats

2 **cups** crispy rice cereal

2 **cups** ground flaxseed meal

1½ **cups** honey

⅔ **cup** sweetened coconut flakes

¼ **cup** coconut oil, optional

4 **teaspoons** vanilla extract

1⅓ **cups (10-ounce bag)** mini chocolate chips

1   In a large mixing bowl, mix the nut butter, old-fashioned oats, steel-cut oats, cereal, flaxseed meal, honey, coconut flakes, coconut oil (if using), and vanilla. Make sure everything is mixed well so that you can easily form the balls later. Mix in the chocolate chips, if using. Chill the mixture in the fridge for an hour so that the balls will hold together.

2   Take a heaping tablespoon portion of the mixture and roll into a ball about 1 inch in diameter. Repeat to make about 24 balls. Store in a gallon-size ziplock bag or sealed container in the freezer for up to a month.

tip For variation you can substitute raisins for chocolate chips or add up to 3 tablespoons chia seeds. We always make a double batch! ✎

Lemon Curd Chia Seed Pudding

Add a zing to your chia seed pudding with this family-favorite recipe! The rich and sweet lemon curd is our favorite complement to the freshness of creamy vanilla chia seed pudding. Top individual servings with fresh fruit, coconut flakes, granola, and more. We love having this pudding on hand for after-school snacks, but it also travels nicely. Kristin often transports a huge batch to the high school for her daughter's dance team during rehearsals, and everyone immediately asks for it again! Store any leftovers in an airtight container for up to seven days.

SERVES 12

32 ounces vanilla Greek yogurt (see Tip)
2 cups favorite milk (almond or coconut)
⅓ cup chia seeds
¼ cup lemon curd

Favorite toppings
   raspberries, strawberries, blueberries, bananas, coconut

Combine the yogurt, milk, chia seeds, and lemon curd in a bowl and mix well. Cover and refrigerate for a couple of hours or overnight. When you are ready to serve, portion the chia pudding into individual serving dishes, and add any toppings you'd like (the possibilities are endless) and enjoy!

tip Kristin uses Dannon Vanilla Light + Fit Greek Yogurt and serves with her homemade Mix and Match Crunchy Granola (see page 49).

Chunky Monkey Oatmeal Pancakes

Our kids tend to get hungry thirty minutes after eating—but not when we make these hearty pancakes! Laurie's friend Lisa Johnson shared this recipe years ago and since then it has become a family favorite. Now our mom loves making these whenever grandchildren come to visit, and they love waking up to their buttery smell! Heating up the griddle and flipping pancakes together—and of course using the batter to make some Mickey Mouse-shaped pancakes—turns breakfast into the happiest meal on Earth!

MAKES 12–16

1½ **cups** all-purpose flour
1½ **cups** quick-cooking oats
2¼ **cups** buttermilk
3 large eggs
¾ **cup** milk

¼ **cup** plus **2 tablespoons** vegetable oil
3 **tablespoons** sugar
1½ **teaspoons** baking soda
1½ **teaspoons** salt

1   Heat an electric griddle to 350°F, or place a cast-iron griddle over medium-high heat and heat for about 3 minutes, until hot.

2   In a large bowl, mix together all the ingredients until slightly lumpy—don't overstir.

3   In ¼-cup portions, drop the batter onto the griddle to make four pancakes at a time. Cook until bubbles appear on the surface of the pancakes, the edges begin to look dull, and the bottoms are golden brown, about 3 minutes. Flip the pancakes and cook until the other sides are golden brown, 2 to 3 minutes longer. Top with butter and your favorite syrup. Enjoy!

tip This batter works great if it is made ahead of time and stored in the fridge overnight. Some of our favorite toppings are chunky applesauce, syrup, and bananas.

Easy Shakshuka

Part of the beauty of traveling the globe and inviting people from other cultures into your home is the new recipes and flavors you add to your world. After enjoying this traditional dish in Israel, we knew we had to duplicate it at home. There's something so warming about the fragrant spices, fresh tomatoes, and runny eggs. Serve with a hunk of crusty bread and it's a meal. It's a repeat for Sunday dinners, 4th of July breakfasts, and ladies' brunches.

SERVES 8

1 tablespoon extra-virgin olive oil
1 onion, chopped
1 sweet red pepper, chopped
3 tablespoons minced garlic
4 (14-ounce) cans fire-roasted diced
   tomatoes with garlic
1 (24-ounce) jar tomato sauce
1 tablespoon ground cumin

1 tablespoon paprika
Dash of cayenne pepper
Salt & ground black pepper to taste
8 large eggs
Optional toppings
   cilantro, parsley, or basil; feta or goat
   cheese; red pepper flakes

1 Heat the olive oil in a cast-iron skillet or large sauté pan over medium heat. Add the onion and red pepper and sauté until translucent, about 8 to 10 minutes. Add the garlic and stir for a minute or two, until aromatic. Add the diced tomatoes, tomato sauce, cumin, paprika, cayenne, and salt and pepper (to taste). Bring to a boil, reduce the heat to a simmer, and cook until slightly thickened, about 10 minutes.

2 With a spoon, make eight large indentations in the sauce. Crack one egg into each divot and cover the pan. Cook over medium heat about 6 to 8 minutes or until the eggs are done to your liking.

3 Remove the pan from the heat, add toppings of your choice, and serve.

Protein Boost Shake for Two

We are creatures of habit and our mantra is, *If it's not broken, why fix it?* This protein shake has been a post-workout snack and the start to Kristin's and Jeremy's day for the past ten years! Now it's a staple in all of our routines, whether we are at home or visiting each other. It's packed with plenty of whole and fresh ingredients, flavor, and lots of protein to keep you full longer. It's delicious, healthy, and if you only eat bread the rest of the day, you're still winning!

SERVES 2

1 **cup** almond milk

2 **scoops** chocolate or vanilla protein powder

2 **scoops** Green Vibrance powder

2 **scoops** collagen powder

1 banana, sliced

¾ **cup** frozen blueberries

2 **big handfuls** greens (spinach, kale, or a mix)

1 **to 2 heaping tablespoons** almond butter

1 **(24-ounce) cup** of ice

In a blender, combine all the ingredients. Blend for 30 seconds. Add the ice and blend again, until thick and smooth.

tip We make protein shake bags and freeze them for quick-and-easy shakes any morning. Add all ingredients except the almond milk and ice to a gallon ziplock bag, making sure the almond butter goes in last, and freeze for up to a month. To serve from frozen, first add the almond milk to the blender and then the frozen ingredients. Blend. Then add ice and finish blending.

Mix and Match Crunchy Granola

Once you taste the unexpected salty-sweet crunch of this flavorful homemade granola, you'll gladly ditch the store-bought version! We've been making our own—and keeping it stocked in our pantries—ever since Kristin's friend Suzette Baird brought over a huge sheet pan of homemade granola and introduced Kristin to the idea of making her own. Baked on the Traeger for a wood-fired kiss, this version is easily customizable, so add your favorite things and omit anything you don't like. We love adding it to yogurt or enjoying it with milk, adding it to cereal, or munching on it plain for a delicious snack.

SERVES 24

11 cups old-fashioned oats
3 cups slivered almonds
2 cups sweetened coconut flakes
⅓ cup flaxseeds
1 cup pecan pieces (or any other nuts)
1 teaspoon cinnamon

1 teaspoon salt
1 cup vegetable oil
1 cup honey
¾ cup packed brown sugar
1 to 2 tablespoons vanilla extract

1 Preheat the oven to 350°F. Mix the oats, almonds, coconut flakes, flaxseeds, pecans, cinnamon, and salt in a large mixing bowl.

2 In a saucepan over low heat, combine the oil, honey, brown sugar, and vanilla and heat through. Add to the bowl of dry ingredients and mix well.

3 Spread the granola evenly on a 11x17-inch baking sheet. Bake for 15 minutes, or until starting to brown. Stir the granola around on the baking sheet and bake for 10 more minutes, until toasted but not burned.

4 Store in a sealed airtight container for up to one month.

CHAPTER 2

Let's Get This Party Started

Growing up, our favorite place to vacation was Hawaii. At our hotel, our parents were invited to enjoy "free" afternoon hors d'oeuvres, so before we went to dinner as a family, us Moore children would sneak in alongside them to try the assortment: elaborate charcuterie boards, canapés, and fresh seafood. We loved the whole experience! Now as adults, when we indulge in our Hawaiian-influenced, **Sesame Ahi Tuna and Avocado Bowl (see page 61)** or Tiffany's **Avocado Shrimp Salsa (see page 53)** we are transported back to those special childhood moments.

Whether we were at a family dinner on the back patio overlooking the hills of Walnut Creek or attending a fancy Christmas soirée (thrown by our parents!), there was always something about appetizers that felt special. In fact, re-inventing appetizers has even become a Moore family tradition! One summer, Danielle and her husband, Parin (our family's culinary genius), spent many hot afternoons outside, sipping on their favorite drinks and watching the kids swim outside, while wearing plastic gloves and trying to avoid jalapeño oil squirting in their eyes, all in the pursuit of perfecting their **Fired-Up Jalapeño Poppers (see page 65)**!

Perhaps it is memories of lounging by the pool with our friends while eating Mom's **Best-Ever Melty Bean Dip (see page 71)**, that infuses us with a general appreciation for the art of a good dip! Our **Pesto and Tomato Brie Dip (see page 66)** has been a holiday staple and is deceptively easy to make. Our **Creamy Whipped Feta Dip (see page 56)** is easily made ahead, scaled up, and adapted to a variety of toppings. And Danielle's version of a viral recipe, **Whipped Goat Cheese with Bacon and Dates (see page 73)** is pretty much the life of the party!

Here you will find an appetizer for every occasion, from backyard bashes (try Kristin's **Super Nachos on page 55**) to elevated dinner parties (try our **Pear, Prosciutto, and Goat Cheese Stacks on page 68**). There is a flavor combination for every palette!

Avocado Shrimp Salsa

This salsa, dip, or eat-it-by-the-spoonful guacamole of yumminess is found at almost all our parties and gatherings. David and Miriam, our number one shrimp fans, make it all the time, for any occasion! It has fresh and bright flavors and is even better the next day, particularly with a sprinkle of our homemade **Smoked Citrus Salt (see page 138)**. Serve with tortilla chips for dipping, on top of rice, or on the side of a protein. It's loved by adults, kids, and shrimp-haters alike!

SERVES 12

Juice of 3 limes
1 tablespoon salt
1 teaspoon ground black pepper
1 teaspoon garlic powder
1 teaspoon onion powder
1 (16-ounce) bag frozen, cooked shrimp, thawed and cut into bite-size pieces
1 cup cooked Persian cucumbers, diced
1 Roma tomato, seeded and diced

1 yellow bell pepper, seeded and diced
½ cup chopped fresh cilantro
¼ cup sliced scallions or minced red onion
4 ripe avocados, seeded, peeled, and diced
Pinch of red pepper or chili flakes, optional
Tortilla chips or Frito scoops for serving

1   Combine the lime juice, salt, black pepper, garlic powder, and onion powder in a small bowl.

2   In a medium bowl, combine the shrimp, cucumber, tomato, bell pepper, cilantro, and scallions and mix. Add the lime juice mixture, then lightly fold in the avocado so the pieces stay intact (more for presentation than anything).

3   Sprinkle everything with red pepper, if you like, and serve with tortilla chips or Frito scoops. David, who loves spice, always adds chili flakes!

Super Nachos

With over three million views on Instagram, Kristin's Super Nachos are famous—and for good reason! Not only are they inexpensive, but with the spectrum of colors and textures from the scallions, jalapeños, and chunky avocado, they are also a visual showstopper! This flavorful crowd-pleaser is simply a whole lot of fun to gather around and enjoy with friends and family. Warning: They will go fast!

SERVES 6–8

2 **cups** cooked pulled pork, bite-size chicken or steak, or your favorite protein

2 **(15-ounce) bags** corn tortilla chips

1 **large block (2 pounds)** sharp cheddar cheese, shredded (shred the cheese yourself for the best results)

1 **(19-ounce) can** black beans (about **2 cups**), rinsed and drained

1 **small jar** of pickled jalapeño slices, drained

1 **cup** pico de gallo or your favorite salsa

½ **cup** roughly chopped fresh cilantro

¼ **cup** chopped scallions

1 **cup** sour cream

2 avocados, pitted, peeled, and diced, or **2 cups** guacamole

2 limes, cut into wedges (optional)

1 Preheat your Traeger grill to 350°F for 15 minutes with the cover on or preheat your oven to 350°F.

2 Place your chosen protein in a flame-proof 11x17-inch baking pan or dish. Place the pan directly on the grill grates, close the lid, and cook until your chosen protein is warmed through, about 15 minutes.

3 Line a rimmed baking sheet with parchment or butcher paper for easy cleanup. Build the nachos on the baking sheet starting with a layer of chips, then evenly disperse half the shredded cheese, half your chosen protein, and half the beans. Top with another layer of chips, cheese, your chosen protein, and beans. Place the baking sheet directly on the grill grate or in the middle of the oven and cook until the cheese is melted, 10 to 15 minutes.

4 Top with the jalapeños, pico de gallo, cilantro, scallions, sour cream, and avocado, and finish off with a squirt of lime, if desired. Enjoy!

Creamy Whipped Feta Dip

Our family just loves to dip! Whether it's on the dance floor or for an appetizer, we are all about the dip, baby, dip. Once you try this whipped feta with yogurt and lemon, we promise you'll love dipping just as much as we do! Serve traditionally or experiment with toppings such as pistachios, mint, or pine nuts. Just be sure to have enough pita chips, crostini, or crunchy toasted baguettes on hand—you'll want to wipe this bowl clean.

SERVES 8–10

1 (8-ounce) block quality feta cheese, drained
¾ cup Greek yogurt
Grated zest of **1** lemon

2 tablespoon extra-virgin olive oil, or more as needed
1 (16-ounce) bag sea salt pita chips (or see Tip, page 62)

In the bowl of a large food processor fitted with a blade (or in a blender), combine the feta, yogurt, and lemon zest and blend. While the processor is running, drizzle the olive oil through the top opening, until the feta is whipped to a smooth mixture. Transfer the whipped feta to a serving plate and serve with pita chips or pita wedges.

Toppings
Go to town with any of these singular toppings or combos: red pepper flakes, chopped fresh mint, chopped fresh parsley, toasted pine nuts, crushed pistachios, hot pepper jelly.

Additional Combos
olive oil + za'atar + pine nuts + kalamata olives
Granny Smith apple + crushed pecans + honey
honey (or hot honey) + everything but the bagel seasoning
grilled peaches (or just sliced peaches!) + balsamic glaze
sliced avocado + everything but the bagel seasoning
prosciutto + basil + fresh cracked black pepper
over-easy egg + everything but the bagel seasoning
sliced strawberries + balsamic glaze (or honey) + chia seeds

Stuffed Mushroom Poppers

Our Aunt Nellie has been making these savory stuffed mushrooms—a legacy from her mother, our Grandma Ruth—for as long as we can remember. Now she brings them over from her home in Long Beach whenever she visits Tiffany in L.A. They are savory, salty, full of flavor, and leave you totally satisfied. These stuffed mushroom poppers are almost a meal in one bite and the perfect go-to for a hearty, crowd-pleasing appetizer.

SERVES 10

1 (16-ounce) container fresh whole mushrooms, wiped clean, stems separated from the caps
⅓ pound bacon
8 tablespoons (1 stick) salted butter

1 small or medium yellow onion, chopped
¼ cup Italian breadcrumbs
¼ cup grated Parmesan cheese

1   Preheat the oven to 350°F.

2   Chop the mushroom stems and set aside. In a skillet over medium heat, cook the bacon until crisp. Drain on paper towels and break into small pieces.

3   In a medium skillet, melt 4 tablespoons of the butter over medium heat. Add the chopped mushroom stems and onion and cook until the moisture is released, about 5 minutes. Add the breadcrumbs, bacon pieces, and Parmesan. Cook and stir until the mixture holds together, about 3 to 5 minutes. Turn the mushroom caps over and fill the cavities with the breadcrumb mixture until slightly overfilled.

4   Melt the remaining 4 tablespoons butter in a small pot over low heat. Dip each stuffed mushroom cap in the melted butter to coat and place on a large baking sheet. Bake the mushrooms until golden brown, about 30 minutes. Pull them out of the oven, place them on a wide platter, and serve!

Sesame Ahi Tuna and Avocado Bowl

Don't let the gourmet look or name of this appetizer fool you—it's so easy to make! We love ahi tuna, and we've found that it's a common item at grocery store salad bars, meaning a portion of the dish is ready to go! This Hawaiian-inspired dish is a favorite recipe of ours for a weeknight meal and is always devoured at potlucks. The reduced soy glaze is the secret sauce that adds the magic to this spectacular appetizer. Layer on a platter and serve with serving spoons.

SERVES 8–10

Soy Glaze
1 cup soy sauce
½ cup sugar

6 to 8 ounces ahi tuna, cut into bite-size pieces
3 tablespoons soy sauce
2 tablespoons toasted sesame oil
3 scallions, sliced
1 tablespoon sesame seeds
3 cups cooked brown rice
2 avocados, pitted, peeled, and smashed
Sriracha, to taste
¼ cup French's crispy fried onions

1 *For the Soy Glaze:* In a small saucepan, simmer 1 cup of soy sauce with ½ cup of sugar. Let simmer for 45 minutes or until reduced to desired consistency. Let cool.

2 *For the Bowl:* In a small bowl, mix the tuna with soy sauce, sesame oil, scallions, and sesame seeds. Set aside to marinate for at least 20 minutes.

3 On a platter, spread the rice to make a flat layer. Spread the avocado on top, followed by the tuna. Finish off with the Soy Glaze and Sriracha, if desired. Top with fried onion pieces and serve.

Greek Seven-Layer Dip

This Mediterranean-inspired twist on a traditional seven-layer bean dip is a lighter alternative for more health-conscious eaters. Packed with fresh vegetables and brought together with your favorite hummus, this dip is easy enough for kids to help assemble and yummy enough that everyone will dig in!

SERVES 8–10

1 **(8-ounce) container** onion and chive cream cheese

1 **(8-ounce) container** Mediterranean or garlic hummus

2 Roma tomatoes, seeded and chopped into very small pieces

1 cucumber, chopped into very small pieces

1 **(small) can** sliced black olives or sliced kalamata olives, drained

3 scallions, sliced

¾ **cup** feta cheese, crumbled

2 **tablespoons** pine nuts, toasted

1 **(16-ounce) bag** sea salt pita chips (or see Tip)

On a medium plate or platter, layer the cream cheese, hummus, tomatoes, cucumber, olives, scallions, and feta. Sprinkle with the toasted pine nuts. Serve with pita chips.

tip   To make your own pita chips, cut 5 pita breads into triangles. Drizzle with olive oil and sprinkle with sea salt. Toast in a 400°F oven, turning once, for about 5 to 8 minutes, until browned on both sides.

Fired-Up Jalapeño Poppers

The heat and sizzle, the smokiness and creaminess—everything about these poppers is the best of the best! On hot summer afternoons, Danielle and her bestie assemble them in the kitchen, seeding jalapeños, filling with cheese, and wrapping them with bacon, before passing them over to Parin to grill. Bring them once to a party, and you'll be asked to bring them again and again! To tone down the heat, make sure to get all of the seeds out of the jalapeños. And don't forget to wear gloves and beware of jalapeño oil squirting into your eyes!

SERVES 12

12 medium jalapeño chiles
8 ounces cream cheese, softened
1 cup shredded cheddar cheese
2 tablespoons garlic salt

24 slices bacon (about **1½ pounds**)
2 tablespoons Traeger Pork & Poultry
    Rub or your favorite smoky rub

1   Preheat your Traeger grill to 350°F for 15 minutes with the cover on or preheat your oven to 350°F.

2   Slice the jalapeños lengthwise in half. Scrape out the seeds and ribs with a small spoon or paring knife. Wear gloves!

3   In a medium bowl, mix together the cream cheese, cheddar cheese, and garlic salt. Spoon the filling into each jalapeño half, then wrap each with one full slice of bacon. Secure with toothpicks.

4   Arrange the jalapeño poppers on a rimmed baking sheet and sprinkle the Traeger rub on top. Place the baking sheet on the grill grates or in the oven and cook for 30 minutes, until the bacon is golden brown and to your desired crispiness. Serve warm.

tip The poppers can be stuffed ahead of time, but wrap with the bacon just before you are ready to cook.

Pesto and Tomato Brie Dip

If you ask any Moore what appetizer has been served the most at family get-togethers or holiday parties, it's this Pesto and Tomato Brie Dip. In fact, it's been in our family since Mom tried it out of the Northgate High School Cookbook over twenty years ago! With peso, fresh tomatoes, and roasted pine nuts elevating the distinct flavor of classic, creamy Brie cheese, you simply can't go wrong!

SERVES 8–10

1 large (8-ounce) round of Brie
1 (8-ounce) container pesto
2 cups large chunks of Roma tomatoes
⅓ cup toasted pine nuts, plus more
   for garnish

½ cup diced scallions, plus a bit more
   for garnish
Crostini crackers or toasted baguette
   slices, for serving

1 Preheat the oven to 350°F.

2 Cut the Brie into small cubes and place in a medium-sized baking dish. Spread the pesto on top, then sprinkle with the tomatoes, pine nuts, and scallions. Mix the ingredients together until combined.

3 Bake for 30 minutes or until bubbling. Stir lightly to work the melted Brie into the pesto and tomatoes. Top with a few more scallions and toasted pine nuts and serve with crackers or toasted baguette slices.

Pear, Prosciutto, and Goat Cheese Stacks

Our parents served these delicious stacks at their annual Christmas party, but the truth is they are simply too good to make only once a year! And though they might look intimidating to prepare, in reality they are the easiest way to add sophistication to a table and give the impression you are an award-winning chef! Crispy prosciutto, creamy goat cheese, and juicy pears create a distinct culinary experience that will bring guests back to the appetizer table again and again.

SERVES 12

6 prosciutto slices, cut in half
2 firm pears
4 **ounces** goat cheese, crumbled
3 **tablespoons** honey

½ **teaspoon** fresh thyme leaves
¼ **teaspoon** coarse salt
½ **teaspoon** ground black pepper

1   Heat the prosciutto in a large skillet over medium-high heat for 2 minutes or until crispy; set aside.

2   Slice the pears horizontally into ¼-inch thin disks. Then carefully take out the centers.

3   Arrange the pear rounds on a platter and top each with a crispy prosciutto piece. Sprinkle with the goat cheese, drizzle with the honey, top with thyme, salt, and pepper, and enjoy!

| tip No crackers needed for this gluten-free app! Add a balsamic glaze to the top for some extra flavor!

Best-Ever Melty Bean Dip

Our family has always loved dip: bean dip, chili dip, queso dip—you name it, we like it! So, naturally, our mom had to elevate our favorite basic bean dip into something more memorable! With grilled onions and corn folded into a creamy base, this ultimate bean dip is fancier and more flavorful than what you may be used to. If you've never raved about a bean dip before, be prepared to rave about this one!

SERVES 8–10

2 **teaspoons** vegetable oil
1 medium onion, sliced
2 **(15-ounce) cans** turkey or beef chili
  with beans
1 **(8-ounce) block** cream cheese,
  at room temperature

1 **(4-ounce) can** green chilies, chopped
1 **cup** frozen corn
1 **cup** shredded cheddar cheese
½ red bell pepper, seeded and chopped
½ **cup** black olives, sliced
Corn chips, for serving

1   Preheat the oven to 350°F.

2   Heat the oil in a skillet over medium heat. Add the onion and sauté until softened and just starting to brown, about 10 minutes. Let cool slightly.

3   Meanwhile, heat the chili in a skillet or saucepan until warmed through. Break the cream cheese into small pieces and mix into the chili until blended. Add the sautéed onions, green chilies, and corn and cook for about 10 minutes, until slightly thickened.

4   Scrape the mixture into a medium shallow baking dish and cover with the cheddar. Bake for 15 to 20 minutes, until the dip is heated through and the cheese is melted.

5   Before serving, sprinkle the dip with the bell pepper and black olives for beautiful color and texture. Serve with corn chips.

Whipped Goat Cheese with Bacon and Dates

When we saw a stunning photograph online of this recipe by Half-Baked Harvest, we knew we wanted to re-create our own decadent version. Whether it's the sweet and savory balance or the ooey-gooey burst of flavor, there is something addicting about a savory dip. Served alongside toasted baguette slices or crostini crackers, this whipped goat cheese is an appetizer you'll make again and again!

SERVES 10–12

12 **ounces** thick bacon, cut into small pieces

12 dates, chopped

2 **tablespoons** fresh rosemary, chopped, or 2 **teaspoons** dried rosemary

2 **teaspoons** brown sugar

⅓ **cup** honey, plus more for drizzling

Pinch cayenne pepper

2 **(10-ounce) logs** creamy goat cheese, room temperature

1 **(8-ounce) package** cream cheese, room temperature

3 **tablespoons** extra-virgin olive oil

1 **teaspoon** salt

2 baguettes, sliced into thin slices and toasted, or crostini crackers

1   Preheat the oven to 325°F.

2   Cook the bacon in a large skillet over medium heat until browned and crispy. Drain the bacon fat and discard, then return the pan to the stove. Add the dates, rosemary, and brown sugar to the bacon and warm through over medium heat for 1 to 2 minutes. Add the honey and a pinch (or more) cayenne to taste.

3   In a large bowl with a hand mixer or food processor, whip together the goat cheese, cream cheese, olive oil, and salt. Transfer the whipped goat cheese mixture to a shallow oven-safe bowl and spoon the bacon and date mixture over the top.

4   Place the goat cheese mixture in the oven. Warm through for 15 minutes or until goat cheese is warm. Remove from oven and then drizzle with additional honey and serve with toast or crackers.

CHAPTER 3

Salad Queen

Mom's reputation as the "Salad Queen" was initiated when the Oakland East Bay Junior League assembled two cookbooks. Inspired by the beautiful recipes, she created **Laurie's Everyday Red Wine Vinaigrette (see page 102)** and that's when the magic started.

While salad had always been at our table, from Grandma Dot's iceberg salad with homemade Thousand Island dressing to a Costco Caesar salad mix, Mom soon began experimenting in combining sweet and savory ingredients and incorporating vegetables and fruits, nuts and cheese.

As more varieties of greens became available in local stores, she experimented with each (Eventually she landed on a favorite—arugula!) Today, Mom's salads incorporate fresh vegetables like heirloom tomatoes, beets, corn, and cucumbers, and fruits like strawberries, pears, peaches, and blueberries, followed by chewy and crunchy elements like dried fruits, candied nuts, and cheeses, and even Kristin's **Homemade Torn Croutons (see page 84)**.

With so many elements balancing one another, we've long since ditched deep salad bowls in favor of platters! In addition to better flavor and texture distribution and ensuring crunchy elements don't turn soggy in the bottom of a bowl, platters display beautifully! Both our **Hearty Fall Salad (see page 89)** and **Niçoise Salad (see page 95)** look particularly stunning with their colorful ingredients lined up on a platter. And our **Peach Burrata and Prosciutto Salad (see page 82)**, with its seared peaches and slices of prosciutto delicately placed on top of lightly tossed greens, can't help but show off!

When David married Miriam, she asked our mom how she makes each salad "work". From that request came Laurie's **Choose Your Own (Salad) Adventure (see page 105)**. Categories, columns, and recommendations help even the most novice salad maker assemble elaborate masterpieces!

Watermelon and Feta Summer Salad

Ten years ago, Kristin created a cookbook for Traeger, *My Summer Table*, consisting of new recipes to share with the Traeger team. With four young daughters in tow, she borrowed her friend's pool for the photoshoot and brought along completed dishes, including this recipe! This savory watermelon salad, reminiscent of barbecues on hot afternoons with watermelon juice running down toddlers' chins, has since become a summer staple.

SERVES 6–8

1 (5-ounce) bag arugula
3 cups seeded watermelon chunks
½ cup feta cheese, crumbled
½ cup sliced tamed jalapeños, drained

Extra-virgin olive oil
Balsamic glaze
Ground black pepper

Spread the arugula on a platter and sprinkle the watermelon, feta, and jalapeños on top. Top with drizzles of olive oil and balsamic glaze, then sprinkle with ground pepper.

The Ultimate Wedge Salad

We always serve our salads on large platters instead of in salad bowls to avoid toppings falling to the bottom. That's especially important for this wedge salad! You want all those tomatoes, chopped hard-boiled eggs, and bacon crumbles to be easy to grab with each wedge so that every bite is balanced! Grab a large platter and make a statement with this easy and elegant salad. Serve these delicious wedges for a weeknight dinner or a potluck and just watch them disappear!

SERVES 16

⅓ purple onion, thinly sliced

3 tablespoons Laurie's Everyday Red Wine Vinaigrette (page 102)

2 heads iceberg lettuce, cut into 8 wedges

2 cups chopped Roma tomatoes

4 hard-boiled eggs, chopped

1 cup crumbled cooked bacon

½ **cup** blue cheese, crumbled

½ **cup** Laurie's Everyday Red Wine Vinaigrette (page 102)

¾ **cup** ranch or blue cheese dressing

2 teaspoons ground black pepper

1   Combine the sliced onion and vinaigrette in a small bowl and marinate for 20 minutes.

2   You will want to use a large platter or dish (not a bowl) for this salad. Arrange the iceberg wedges (keep them in wedge form) across your platter. Top with tomatoes, hard-boiled eggs, bacon, marinated onion, and blue cheese.

3   Drizzle both the vinaigrette and ranch or blue cheese dressing in zig-zags across salad. Top with a heavy hand of ground pepper.

Macho Salad

This salad has been requested for more birthdays, luncheons, dinner parties, and weeknight meals than we can count! Inspired by our favorite salad at Banderas in Corona del Mar, it is loved by everyone who tries it. This colorful masterpiece has so many delicious elements that harmonize together to create the perfect bite. Fragrant Dijon mustard and balsamic vinaigrette complement the chewy dates, fresh corn, and crunchy **Cornbread Croutons (see page 84)**. We are convinced it's the perfect salad!

SERVES 10–12

Vinaigrette
¾ **cup** extra-virgin olive oil
¼ **cup** fresh lemon juice
1½ **tablespoons** Dijon mustard
2 **teaspoons** light brown sugar
1 **teaspoon** balsamic vinegar
2 **cloves** garlic, minced
½ **teaspoon** dried oregano
¼ **teaspoon** dried basil
½ **teaspoon** kosher salt
¼ **teaspoon** ground black pepper

Salad
6 **cups** romaine or red leaf lettuce or a mix, chopped
1½ **pounds** shredded rotisserie chicken
1 avocado, pitted, peeled, and chopped
2 whole large Roma tomatoes, seeded and coarsely chopped
1 **cup** frozen corn, heated through, or fresh corn from the cob
1 **cup** sliced dates (from **12 to 14** whole dates)
½ **cup** toasted almonds, coarsely chopped
¼ **cup** goat cheese, crumbled
1 **cup** cornbread croutons (page 84)

1   *For the vinaigrette:* Combine all of the ingredients in a small bowl and whisk until fully combined.

2   *For the salad:* Toss all the ingredients in a large bowl. Toss in the croutons. Add the vinaigrette and mix until everything is fully combined. Serve immediately.

Peach Burrata and Prosciutto Salad

We love the pairing of juicy sliced peaches and creamy burrata cheese in this flavorful salad. The soft crunch of butter lettuce and the crunchy, sweet nuttiness from the pecans all combine into this Moore family staple. Don't skip the French bread croutons, which add a delicious buttery crunch. It's the perfect salad for peach season and you can easily substitute pears during the fall and winter months. The mix of sweet and salty flavors and the variety of ingredients make it the star at most summer gatherings and dinners al fresco.

SERVES 6–8

1 **(10-ounce) bag** arugula

1 **(10-ounce) bag** butter lettuce or spring mix

½ **cup** Laurie's Everyday Red Wine Vinaigrette (page 102)

2 **large (8-ounce) balls** burrata, torn into pieces

5 **pieces** prosciutto

1 large fresh peach, pitted, cut into thin slices, and seared

½ **cup** candied pecans

½ **loaf** French bread, sliced, buttered, torn, and toasted

Balsamic glaze

Toss the arugula and butter lettuce with about ¼ cup vinaigrette. On a large platter, arrange the greens, then top with the burrata, prosciutto, seared peaches, and pecans. Add the French bread croutons and drizzle with a little more vinaigrette and about 2 tablespoons balsamic glaze.

tip For a beautiful sear mark, grill the peach halves directly on a Traeger grill grate at 350°F for 2 to 3 minutes.

Cornbread Croutons

These croutons, a little chewy inside and crispy outside, improve just about any salad! You'll need dense, heavy, buttery cornbread here, so buy pre-made cornbread at your grocery store. You can also use leftovers from our **Skillet Cornbread recipe (see page 159)** if you happen to have any!

1   Preheat the oven to 325°F.

2   Cut cornbread into 1-inch squares and arrange on a baking sheet. Drizzle with olive oil and sprinkle on a little kosher salt.

3   Bake at 325°F for 15 to 20 minutes, or until starting to get golden brown. Mix around and bake for 5 more minutes, until golden brown.

4   Remove from oven and let cool. Use to top your favorite salads.

Homemade Torn Croutons

Once you make homemade croutons, we promise you will never go back to store-bought! They elevate any salad. This recipe is simple and versatile—you can use any type of bread that tears well without crumbling! We love using loaves of sourdough, French, or ciabatta. The hardest part of this recipe is trying not to eat them all before you've made the salad!

1   Tear your favorite bread into bite-size pieces.

2   Arrange the torn bread on a baking sheet, generously drizzle extra-virgin olive oil all over, and then season with salt.

3   Bake at 350°F until crisp, tossing after 5 minutes to brown all sides.

Apple Pecan Salad

Laurie has friends over for lunch often and is constantly trying new flavor combinations and sharing her recipes! This Apple Pecan Salad includes all of our favorite ingredients—dried fruit, cheese, peppers—which we pack in by the handful, but is chameleon-like in its ability to adapt to a variety of flavor profiles and textures. Feel free to join in by dumping on loads of your favorite toppings or cutting back on others—we promise it will turn out delicious!

SERVES 12

6 apples, cored and chopped

1 small red bell pepper, seeded and chopped

¼ **cup** dried cranberries

¼ **cup** golden raisins

1¼ **cup** Laurie's Everyday Red Wine Vinaigrette (page 102)

1 (10-ounce) **bag** butter lettuce

1 (10-ounce) **bag** arugula

¾ **cup** shredded Swiss cheese

½ **cup** candied pecans

¼ **cup** pomegranate seeds

1   In a large bowl, combine the apples, bell pepper, cranberries, and raisins. Add about 1 cup vinaigrette and marinate while preparing the rest of the salad.

2   In a separate bowl, mix together the butter lettuce and arugula and ¼ cup vinaigrette.

3   Arrange the greens on one large serving platter or individual salad plates, then top with the fruit mixture. Top with the cheese, candied pecans, and pomegranate. Serve immediately and enjoy!

tip When persimmons are in season, we use them in place of apples. Persimmons combine the tangy and sweet flavors of mangoes and sweet peppers with a subtle touch of warm spice.

Hearty Fall Salad

We love this heartwarming fall salad for its rich flavors and autumn colors—something about the glazed squash and maple syrup just seems to pair beautifully with the changing leaves and crisp cool air! This salad feels intentional and elevated, so Laurie loves serving this at ladies' lunches. Bulked up with wild rice, butternut squash, and Brussels sprouts, it is filling enough to serve alone or as a complement to your main dish. Serve with a rotisserie chicken...and dinner is done!

SERVES 10–12

2 **cups** wild rice blend (or see Tips)
2 **cups** cubed butternut squash
Extra-virgin olive oil, for drizzling
1 **tablespoon** brown sugar
1 **tablespoon** salt
½ **teaspoon** ground black pepper
2 **cups** thinly sliced Brussels sprouts
1 **(5-ounce) bag** arugula
⅔ **cup** dried cherries
1 **cup** pecans, toasted

Maple Vinaigrette
1 **cup** extra-virgin olive oil
3 **tablespoons** apple cider vinegar
½ **cup** balsamic vinegar
¼ **cup** maple syrup
1 **tablespoon** Dijon mustard
Salt & ground black pepper, to taste

1   Preheat the oven to 425°F.

2   Cook the wild rice blend according to package directions.

3   Place the cubed butternut squash on a baking sheet, drizzle with about 1 to 2 tablespoons olive oil. Sprinkle with the brown sugar, salt, and pepper and then toss. Roast the butternut squash for 30 to 40 minutes, until browned and tender.

4   Spread the Brussels sprouts on a second baking sheet, drizzle with a generous amount of olive oil, and sprinkle with salt and pepper. Roast the sprouts in the oven along with the squash for 10 to 15 minutes, until browned and crispy.

5 On a deep platter, line up the rice, butternut squash, Brussels sprouts, dried cherries, and pecans over the arugula.

6 *To make the maple vinaigrette:* Combine all the vinaigrette ingredients and whisk to emulsify.

7 Pour the desired amount of vinaigrette over the salad and let sit for 10 minutes before serving. This salad is just as good the next day!

tip Pre-made, microwavable wild rice packets work really well in this recipe. And don't hesitate to pick up packaged pre-sliced Brussels sprouts or pre-chopped butternut squash.

Baked Pear
and Goat Cheese Salad

You can't get more elegant than our baked pear salad. An ode to the classic dinner party, Laurie still loves to plate this salad for a nice sit-down dinner. The composition is visually stunning, and a separate salad course draws out the meal, allowing all to savor the moment of being together. The pear, dried fruits, nuts, and cheese combination, baked and then served on a layer of your favorite lettuce, is not only elegant, but tastes fabulous. Your salad will be the talk of the night! To serve a crowd, assemble baked pears together on a platter.

SERVES 10

¼ **cup** dried cranberries

¼ **cup** golden raisins

¼ **cup** roasted pecan pieces, chopped

10 ounces honey goat cheese or gorgonzola (your preference), room temperature

5 ripe pears, halved and cored

Cinnamon

1 (7-ounce) bag arugula or any lettuce

Laurie's Everyday Red Wine Vinaigrette (page 102)

Maple syrup

1 Combine the cranberries, raisins, and pecans with the softened cheese. Chill.

2 Set the Traeger grill to 375°F or preheat the oven to 375°F.

3 Place the pear halves in a baking pan, hollow sides up. With oiled hands, form 10 balls from the cheese mixture and place in the hollow of the pears. Lightly dust each pear with dashes of cinnamon. Bake the filled pears in the oven or covered grill for 20 minutes, until golden brown.

4 Divide the arugula among individual salad plates, or place all on a large platter. Place the filled pears on top of the arugula, drizzle with vinaigrette, and dollop with maple syrup before serving!

Niçoise Salad

While pregnant with David, Laurie and Doug took a "babymoon" to the South of France. Staying in a turret room in the hillside town of St. Paul de Vence, they tried their first Niçoise salad, a regional specialty. So, of course, when they returned home, Laurie recreated it! We now use seared ahi instead of flake tuna for our Niçoise and it has become a Sunday night favorite. And when we serve this at parties on a large platter, it's gone in a blink! Bon appétit!

SERVES 12–14

Niçoise Vinaigrette
½ cup extra-virgin olive oil
3 tablespoons red wine vinegar
Juice of ½ lemon
1 tablespoon Dijon mustard
¼ cup chopped fresh flat-leaf parsley
2 cloves garlic, minced (frozen garlic cubes from Trader Joe's work too)
1 tablespoon minced fresh tarragon leaves (use **1 teaspoon** dried if you don't have fresh)
1 teaspoon maple syrup
½ teaspoon salt
¼ teaspoon ground black pepper

Salad
1 pound small, red, new potatoes, quartered
Extra-virgin olive oil
Salt & ground black pepper
½ pound green beans, stems trimmed
2 pounds fresh sushi-quality ahi tuna (see Tip)
Your favorite lettuce (we love red leaf, butter, or spring mix)
1 pint teardrop or cherry tomatoes, halved
8 large hard-boiled eggs, sliced
1 cup Greek olives

1 *For the vinaigrette:* Combine all the ingredients in a small bowl and whisk to emulsify.

2 *For the salad:* Preheat the oven to 350°F.

3 In a bowl, drizzle the potatoes with 2 tablespoons olive oil, season with 1 teaspoon salt, and toss to coat. Arrange on a medium baking sheet and bake until fork-tender, about 30 minutes.

4 On a separate medium baking sheet, drizzle the beans with olive oil and season with a dash of salt and pepper. Bake along with the potatoes for 10 to 12 minutes, until al dente.

5 Rub the tuna with olive oil and a good amount of salt and pepper. Heat a large skillet over high heat until very hot. Lay the tuna in the hot skillet and sear for about 2 minutes, turning once, until browned. Transfer to a plate and cool for 5 minutes, then cut into bite-size chunks with a sharp knife. Mix the tuna with a few tablespoons of the vinaigrette.

6 Lightly toss green beans, tomatoes, and potatoes with dressing to coat. Cover a large platter with lettuce. Place the potatoes, beans, tomatoes, eggs, and olives in clumps on top of the lettuce (rather than spreading across the salad). Serve the remaining vinaigrette on the side.

| tip This salad is great with grilled salmon or steak as well!

Thai Steak Salad with Toasted Sesame Dressing

As empty nesters, one of Laurie and Doug's favorite traditions is to drive to Napa on the weekend for lunch at R&D Kitchen, where they often order the Thai Steak Salad. However, on hot summer days when they don't want to leave the house, they enjoy their own leisurely lunch in the shade of their patio and recreate this salad themselves! Light and flavorful, this salad is great for warm-weather entertaining because you can make it ahead of time and serve at room temp, not to mention that it looks amazing on a platter, serves a lot of people, and is a great use of leftover pasta and/or steak.

SERVES 8–10

Salad
1 pound flank or tri-tip steak
1 cup teriyaki sauce or soy sauce
1 (16-ounce) package spaghetti
Extra-virgin olive oil
1 (10-ounce) bag cabbage or arugula
1 (10-ounce) bag shredded carrots
2 to 3 mangoes, pitted, peeled, and cubed
1 orange or red bell pepper, seeded and chopped
1 bunch scallions, thinly sliced
½ bunch fresh cilantro, chopped

12 Thai basil leaves, chopped
2 cups store-bought toasted sesame dressing (or make your own, below)
½ cup honey-roasted peanuts

Toasted Sesame Dressing
½ cup soy sauce
½ cup white vinegar
½ cup tahini
½ cup peanut butter
¼ cup toasted sesame oil
2 tablespoons honey

1 In a large bowl, marinate the steak in the teriyaki sauce or soy sauce for one hour in the fridge. Drain before grilling.

2 Cook the pasta according to package directions until al dente. Strain the pasta and toss with a dash of olive oil to keep noodles separated.

3 Preheat the Traeger grill to 225°F. Place the steak directly on the grill grate and

cook, turning once, until the internal temperature reaches 135°F for medium-rare, about 10 minutes per side. Let the meat rest for 15 minutes and then thinly slice.

4 *To make the homemade sesame dressing:* In a small bowl, mix together ½ cup soy sauce, ½ cup white vinegar, ½ cup tahini, ½ cup peanut butter, ¼ cup toasted sesame oil, and 2 tablespoons honey.

5 In a large bowl, mix the cabbage, carrots, bell pepper, mangoes, scallions, cilantro, and basil, reserving some scallions and red peppers for garnish. Add the noodles to the bowl and toss again. Pour the dressing over the mixture and toss well to combine.

6 Arrange the pasta salad on a platter, top with the sliced steak, and garnish with the remaining peppers and scallions and the peanuts.

Salad de Maison

If you're looking for a salad easy enough to serve on repeat multiple times a week and yummy enough to never tire of, then this is the salad for you! The simple components—fresh garlic, peppery arugula, and crunchy slivered almonds—make it the perfect side to any meal and easy to assemble in a pinch. While Kristin makes it often, it wasn't until Jeremy began making it alongside his famous **Reverse-seared Filet Mignon (see page 126)** that it claimed a coveted spot in the Andrus family's weekly rotation!

SERVES 6

Dressing
½ **cup** extra-virgin olive oil
⅓ **cup** fresh lemon juice
2 garlic cloves, diced finely
½ **teaspoon** salt
¼ **teaspoon** coarse ground pepper

Salad
½ **cup** slivered almonds
1 **(5-ounce) bag** arugula
¼ **cup** grated Parmesan cheese

1 In a mason jar or bowl, combine the olive oil, lemon juice, garlic, salt, and pepper and mix well. Let sit.

2 In a small, dry sauté pan over medium heat, sauté the slivered almonds until toasty brown, about 4 to 6 minutes.

3 In a medium bowl, toss together the arugula, Parmesan, and almonds. Add desired amount of dressing to salad, mix well, and serve!

tip We always toast nuts in bulk, then store in a ziplock bag in our freezer to use in a pinch. The dressing saves well in the fridge and can be used on a variety of salads as well as vegetables, chicken, and fish. ✎

Laurie's Everyday Red Wine Vinaigrette

We have such a hard time keeping this vinaigrette on hand in our fridges because we use it so often! It is delicious on all kinds of savory or sweet salads and even drizzled on vegetables. Dice the red onion very small and sit back as the onion marinates in the red wine vinegar, compounding the flavor. Since we use this recipe all the time, we always end up with plenty of requests for this recipe—it is truly loved by all who try it.

MAKES 2 CUPS

1 cup extra-virgin olive oil
½ cup red wine vinegar
¼ cup finely diced red/purple onion
3 tablespoons sugar
Salt & ground black pepper to taste

Combine all the ingredients in a mason jar or sealed container and shake thoroughly. Best to make at least a day ahead so the onion can marinate. Feel free to double or triple the recipe. It lasts for a long time in the refrigerator.

Choose Your Own (Salad) Adventure

Our mom has always been known as the Salad Queen! She certainly has mastered the art of salads by layering her greens, pairing her toppings, and balancing the crunchy and chewy elements. Whenever she serves a salad, her guests are always impressed with the variation of flavor profiles and textures. When David married Miriam, she asked the secret behind assembling one of Laurie's signature salads—so this salad chart was created. This is the ultimate cheat sheet for becoming the salad queen in your own home.

STEP 1: GREENS

PICK 1 OR MORE
Butter lettuce
Arugula
Baby spinach
Shredded cabbage
Romaine

STEP 2: DECIDE WHAT WILL BE PROMINENT—SWEET OR SAVORY?

SWEET INGREDIENTS—PICK AT LEAST 3

Apple slices	Shredded carrots
Pear slices	Pomegranate seeds
Mango chunks	Berries
Persimmon slices	Jicama slices
Peach slices	Dried cranberries
Fresh orange segments	Golden raisins
Canned mandarin orange segments	Chopped dates
Jarred pink grapefruit segments	Toasted coconut

STEP 2 *continued*

SAVORY INGREDIENTS—PICK AT LEAST 3

Tomato

Avocado cubes

Carrot ribbons

Persian cucumber slices

Hearts of palm

Corn

Peas

Beet slices

Green or black olives

Bell pepper cubes

Roasted potatoes or vegetables

STEP 3: PICK THE OTHER GOODIES

CHEESE—PICK 1

Swiss

Goat cheese

Trader Joe's honey goat cheese

Feta

Monterey jack

Cheddar

Mozzarella

NUTS—PICK 1

Almonds

Pistachios

Honey-roasted or regular peanuts

Pine nuts

Candied pecans

SPECIAL TOUCHES—AS NEEDED

Hard-boiled egg slices

**Homemade Torn Croutons
  (page 84)**

Crispy Asian noodles

French's crispy fried onions

Toasted coconut

TO MAKE IT A MEAL—PICK 1

Shredded chicken breast

Cooked bacon pieces

Tuna or chicken salad

Chopped ham

Grilled pork tenderloin

Ahi tuna (raw or seared)

Baked salmon

Turkey breast

Rice/grains/pasta

Oven-roasted potatoes

STEP 4: PUT IT ALL TOGETHER

Mix greens with a light amount of dressing. (Almost exclusively, we use **Laurie's Everyday Red Wine Vinaigrette, page 102**, on both sweet or savory salads!) Spread the greens on a platter. Mix all vegetables, fruit, protein, and grains with vinaigrette. Top the lettuce with the mixed vegetables or fruit combinations. Garnish with cheese, nuts, and any of the special toppings that you want. We like to combine different textures, so we often add dried cranberries or golden raisins or dates to most of our salads. Finally, garnish with any can't-miss touches if desired, and top with your protein of choice to make it a meal.

CHAPTER 4

Traeger'd Favorites

It is hardly a Moore family gathering without someone firing up the Traeger! "Traegering," as we affectionately call it, is our go-to method for cooking everything from meats and seafood to vegetables and sides. Not only does it simplify cooking for a crowd, but there is something inherently appealing in the art of grilling and smoking!

Long before Traeger, our dad's love of grilling began in his own childhood when he helped pile newspaper bundles and gather sticks. He then learned the process of testing charcoal, mastering accurate temperatures, and perfecting grill marks. As he went away to college and got married, Dad would often take his portable Hibachi grill camping or to the beach. When our parents moved to Kansas City in the late 1970s, they developed their famous Moore Sauce. Embracing the busy years with young children at home, Mom would focus on planning and preparing delicious spreads, while Dad would grill everything from ribs to filet mignon. Grilling was the perfect way for them to divide responsibilities and establish a partnership for seamless hosting.

Years later as a newlywed, Kristin embraced the same tradition, following Dad's example by mastering the craft of good barbecue. Once Kristin and Jeremy bought Traeger, Jeremy's own love of grilling and smoking emerged. His passion has since permeated our entire family! Not long afterward, Jeremy and Dad grilled for the Traeger team using the famous Moore Sauce. Urging Dad to call it something cooler, David reminded Dad of a nickname he'd earned in junior high...Sugar Lips. The sauce was a hit and the name stuck!

Despite the delicious results of Traegering, we are convinced it's the gathering we love most—sharing stories, cooking over a wood fire, and enjoying special moments that come with the smoky, heart-warming, and mouth-watering smell of sizzling barbecue in the air.

Traeger Essentials

A Traeger Wood Pellet Grill is the best way to cook meat, fish, and even veggies for a crowd, and Jeremy and Kristin (and the rest of us) love the ease it brings to our gatherings. Combining features of conventional ovens and traditional grills, Traeger grills can be used to smoke, roast, bake, grill, and sear just about anything. A Traeger grill makes wood-fired cooking simple!

HOW TO USE A TRAEGER GRILL

1 Start with a clean grill.

2 Fill the hopper with your favorite Traeger pellets.

3 Prepare your food (and season it with a Traeger rub).

4 Choose the right grill temperature and preheat your grill.

5 Use the "Super Smoke" function if you have it when more wood fired flavor is desired. Super smoke was specifically designed to add even more robust smoke flavor to your low and slow cooks (under 225°F).

6 Use a meat thermometer to monitor internal meat temperature. Remember, always cook to temp, not to time.

7 Smoke the food directly on the grate or use a pan. Any dish that you would cook in an oven, can be used on a Traeger.

8 Keep the grill lid closed during smoking. If you're looking, you ain't cooking.

9 Let smoked meats rest.

TEMPERATURE

Setting the temperature on your Traeger grill is as easy as turning on your oven and anything you can cook on a gas grill, you can cook on a Traeger wood pellet grill. A Traeger grill will transform the way you cook because it creates consistent results, every single time. The ideal grill temperature for smoking food is around 225°F, though some smoking recipes go as low as 165°F and others up to 275°F.

PELLETS

Traeger pellets come in a variety of flavors to suit every type of food. Fruit woods like cherry and apple impart a sweeter, more subtle flavor that matches perfectly with poultry, pork, seafood, and baked goods. Bolder hardwood pellets like oak, hickory, and mesquite are tailor-made for savory beef, wild game, and vegetables. Our favorites are Traeger's Cherry, Pecan, or Signature Blend Wood Pellets.

TRAEGER GRILL VS. OVEN

A Traeger grill acts just like an oven on the convection setting. If a recipe was developed for a non-convection oven, you may want to reduce the temperature on the Traeger by 25 degrees and start checking for doneness sooner.

MEAT TEMPERATURE GUIDELINES

Steak
115°F and below for black & blue
120–125°F for rare
130–135°F for medium-rare
140–145°F for medium
150–155°F for medium-well
160–165°F for well done

Pork
Pork chops 140°F
Pulled pork 204°F
Pork ribs 203°F

Chicken
165°F

Note: Different types of meat should be cooked at different temperatures depending on the size and type of your cut and your cooking method. But, whether you're roasting or grilling, you have to get it to a certain internal temperature before it's safe to serve. The USDA recommended safe serving temperature for your most common cuts starts at 145°F and goes up to around 165°F. Again, this all varies based on the type of meat.

Flank Steak with Chimichurri

Thanks to Kristin constantly experimenting with new ways to elevate familiar food, we all now serve our steak alongside this fresh, vibrant chimichurri sauce topped with juicy pomegranate seeds. It's a cheerful, accessible dish that we return to for everything from holiday parties to Sunday dinners! Adjust the red pepper flakes based on your heat preference, but don't skimp on the chimichurri sauce!

SERVES 4–6

1 **cup** chopped fresh parsley leaves
1 **cup** chopped fresh cilantro leaves
¼ **cup** red wine vinegar
5 **cloves** garlic, peeled (or 5 Trader Joe's frozen garlic cubes)
1 **teaspoon** kosher salt

1 **teaspoon** red pepper flakes
1 **teaspoon** ground black pepper
½ **cup** extra-virgin olive oil
1 **(2-pound)** flank steak
Pomegranate seeds, optional (based on seasonal availability)

1 For the chimichurri, combine the parsley, cilantro, vinegar, garlic, salt, red pepper flakes, and black pepper in a blender and pulse a few times. Slowly pour in the olive oil while pulsing a few more times, until the chimichurri is chunky, but not mushy.

2 Place the flank steak in a ziplock bag and add ½ cup of the chimichurri. Marinate in the refrigerator for 1 to 3 hours. Once it has marinated, remove the flank steak from the refrigerator and let it come to room temperature, about 30 minutes.

3 Preheat the Traeger grill to 450°F for 15 minutes with the lid closed.

4 Remove the steak from marinade, place directly on the grill grates, and close the lid. Cook, turning once, until the internal temperature of the meat reaches 130°F for medium-rare, about 10 minutes per side. Remove the steak from the grill and let rest 15 minutes before slicing.

5 With a sharp knife, slice the steak against the grain as thinly as you can, for the most delicious results. If you have them, add pomegranate seeds to the remaining chimichurri and pour over the sliced flank steak.

Easy Weeknight Chicken Thighs

While Traeger might be known for its smoked ribs and epic brisket, it was actually basic chicken that first introduced Kristin and Jeremy to the transformative effect cooking with wood has on food—enhancing the flavor with a smoky infusion and increasing tenderness with a slow cook. Years ago, curious about the business of Traeger, Jeremy brought home a grill, Kristin marinated the chicken, and once it finished smoking, they turned to each other and said, "That was the best chicken I have ever had!" It's fair to say they've been Traegering ever since!

SERVES 12

12 chicken thighs
Kosher salt
2 tablespoons Traeger Chicken Rub
Ground black pepper

1 Set the Traeger grill to 350°F and preheat with the lid closed for 15 minutes.

2 While the grill is heating, trim any excess fat and skin from the chicken thighs. Season lightly with salt and pepper, then with the chicken rub.

3 Place the chicken thighs directly on the grill grates, close the lid, and cook until the internal temperature reaches 180°F, about 35 minutes. (The chicken will be cooked through at 165°F, but the texture will be better at 180°F.) Remove the chicken from the grill and let rest for a few minutes before serving.

tip For teriyaki chicken thighs, combine the thighs and 1½ cups teriyaki sauce in a large ziplock bag, seal, turn to coat, and marinate for at least 1 hour. Garnish the grilled thighs with sesame seeds and sliced scallions.

Teriyaki Salmon

Served with scallions and sliced citrus on top, this teriyaki salmon is a statement on any dinner table or party spread. It's easily prepared ahead of time, stored in the fridge, and then baked just prior to company arriving. Our sister-in-law Miriam prepares this dish all the time and it has even become a hit with her extended family. Even for people who aren't big fish lovers, this is always popular!

SERVES 6

1 **(3-pound)** salmon fillet, skin removed
1 **cup** apricot jam
1 **cup** teriyaki sauce

3 to 5 dashes soy sauce
1 **bunch** scallions, finely chopped
1 to 2 lemons, thinly sliced

1   Set the Traeger grill to 350°F and preheat with the lid closed for 15 minutes.

2   Mix together apricot jam and teriyaki with 3 to 5 dashes of soy sauce. (The more marinade you use, the saucier the salmon will be. In our opinion, the saucier, the better!) Spread ¼ of the marinade on the bottom of a 9x13-inch disposable aluminum pan. Place the salmon in the pan; if it is too long, fold the salmon over at the narrower thin end. Pour the rest of the marinade over the salmon, top with the sliced scallions, and arrange the citrus slices down the center.

3   Cook in the Traeger (or roast in the oven) until the salmon flakes when pricked with a fork, 20 to 30 minutes, depending upon the thickness of the salmon. Check periodically as to not over bake.

tip   This recipe can be made with smaller salmon fillets. Simply adjust the size of the baking dish and the amount of sauce.

Doug's Famous Baby Back Ribs

There's a reason these ribs are one of our dad's most requested grilling masterpieces. Slow-grilled for hours, then wrapped in foil with apple juice, drizzled with maple syrup, and sprinkled with brown sugar, these ribs aren't finished until Dad has generously basted them with his famous Sugar Lips sauce! Everyone who eats one ends up licking their plate *and* their fingers!

SERVES 6

2 racks baby back pork ribs
3 tablespoons Traeger Coffee Rub or
   your favorite pork or poultry rub
2 cups apple juice or water

½ cup maple syrup
½ cup brown sugar
Traeger Sugar Lips BBQ sauce or your
   favorite BBQ sauce

1   Set the Traeger grill to 180°F. Cover and preheat for 15 minutes.

2   If your butcher has not already done so, remove the thin silverskin membrane from the bone side of the ribs by working the tip of a butter knife or a screwdriver underneath the membrane and grabbing the membrane with a paper towel to pull off. Rub each rack with the rub. Place the racks on the grill, meat side up, cover, and cook for 3 hours.

3   Lay out two oversized sheets of foil and place a rack on each. Form a bowl around each rack with the foil, being careful not to poke holes in the foil. Pour the apple juice or water into the foil bowls. Drizzle the maple syrup in ribbons (back and forth motion) across the top of each rack, then follow with a generous sprinkling of brown sugar. Close the foil bowls very carefully, but also tightly, with no openings.

4   Increase the grill temperature to 225°F. Place the ribs back on the grill and cover and cook for about 2 hours, until the internal temperature is 205°F.

5   Cut each rack into individual ribs and brush with barbecue sauce. Put the ribs back on the grill for 10 to 15 minutes, until caramelized. Then add more sauce.

Million Dollar Bacon

For their eighth annual Fourth of July breakfast, Kristin and Jeremy were looking for a new way to wow guests. By brushing thick-cut bacon with a mixture of maple syrup and brown sugar, then sprinkling it with cayenne pepper before grilling on the Traeger, Kristin elevated this everyday American food into something extraordinary. That first year, someone had to guard the platter so the kids didn't eat it all! "Million Dollar Bacon" is now part of the annual menu, and as Doug and Laurie are usually in town for the Fourth of July, Doug has become known in the Andrus's neighborhood as the bacon grillmaster!

SERVES 8

1 (16-ounce) package thick-cut bacon
½ cup maple syrup
¼ cup brown sugar
1 teaspoon cayenne pepper

1   Set the Traeger grill to 175°F and preheat with the lid closed for 15 minutes.

2   Arrange the bacon slices on a metal cooling rack and place on a foil-lined baking sheet. Drizzle ribbons of maple syrup over the bacon slices, then sprinkle with the brown sugar, which will stick nicely to the bacon because of the maple syrup. Repeat until you have placed all bacon slices on your baking sheets.

3   Place the baking sheets on the grill grates and cover and cook for 10 or 20 minutes, depending on grill temperature, until firm. With tongs, flip the bacon over and cook for 10 or 20 minutes longer, until done. It is critical to watch the bacon for doneness: The thickness of the bacon and grill temperatures vary, so keep watching and checking until you get to know your grill. To finish off, turn the grill up to 375°F and bake until crispy.

Smoky Reverse-Seared Tri-Tip

Parin always recommends this dish to friends who are new to grilling. Tri-tip goes a long way and is nearly impossible to mess up, particularly because it stays tender longer than more sensitive meats! Slow-cooked and then finished with a nice sear, this smoked tri-tip is juicy, flavorful and addicting!

SERVES 5

1 **(3-pound)** tri-tip steak
2 **tablespoons** ground black pepper
2 **tablespoons** kosher salt

1   Remove the tri-tip from the refrigerator and let it come to room temperature, about 45 minutes. When ready to cook, set the Traeger to 205°F and preheat with the lid closed for 15 minutes. For optimal flavor, use the Super Smoke function, if available.

2   In a small bowl, combine the salt and pepper and generously season all sides of the steak. Insert a thermometer probe into the thickest part of the steak. Place the tri-tip directly on the grill grate, close the lid, and cook until the internal temperature reaches 120°F, 60 to 90 minutes. Remove the smoked tri-tip from the grill and wrap in foil.

3   Increase the Traeger temperature to 450°F (or 500°F, if available) and preheat with the lid closed for 15 minutes. Unwrap the steak. Re-insert the probe and return the steak to the grill. Sear on each side for 5 minutes, or until the internal temperature reaches 128°F. Remove the tri-tip from the grill and let rest for 10 to 15 minutes. Slice against the grain, as thinly as possible, then serve.

tip   We often add a Traeger rub, though of course it's flavorful enough on its own! 🥄

Pork Tenderloin with Citrus Chimichurri Sauce

Pork tenderloin remains the number one protein that we cook when we gather people together. Slathered with a zesty, citrusy chimichurri, this dish is memorable, fragrant, and simple enough to keep on repeat! Though we've made changes to the recipe over the years (ever since Kristin's friend Catherine first brought it over nearly twenty years ago!) and have used a variety of different citrus profiles, it always turns out delicious!

SERVES 8–10

4 (1½ lb) pork tenderloins
1 cup extra-virgin olive oil
1 tablespoon grated lime zest, plus
   1 cup fresh juice (from about 4 limes)
1 tablespoon grated orange zest, plus
   ¾ cup fresh juice (from about 1 to 2 oranges)

½ cup chopped fresh cilantro
8 cloves garlic, minced
1 tablespoon dried oregano
1 tablespoon ground cumin
1½ teaspoons salt
1½ teaspoons ground black pepper

1 Rinse and pat dry the tenderloins and place in a gallon ziplock bag. In a bowl, combine the olive oil, lime zest and juice, orange zest and juice, cilantro, garlic, oregano, cumin, salt, and pepper. Add ⅓ of the citrus chimichurri to the pork in the bag, reserving the rest. Seal, turn to coat, and marinate in the refrigerator for at least 2 hours or up to 2 days.

2 Set the Traeger grill to 375°F. Cover and preheat for 15 minutes.

3 Drain the marinade and then place the tenderloins directly on the grill grate and cover and cook for 10 minutes. Flip the loins over and cook for an additional 4 to 8 minutes at 425°F, until the internal temperature reaches 145°F (pork will be slightly pink in the center, do not overcook). Remove the pork from the grill, cover with foil, and let rest for 10 to 15 minutes.

4 Cut the tenderloins into about ⅓-inch-thick slices and arrange, overlapping, on a platter. Spoon the reserved chimichurri sauce over the pork and serve.

Reverse-Seared Filet Mignon

When Traeger's corporate offices were shut down during Covid, Jeremy decided to host business lunch meetings at his house multiple times a week to stay connected to his people. He kept the menu simple and consistent: **Salad de Maison (see page 101)**, **Salt-Crusted Baked Potatoes (see page 157)**, a loaf of sourdough bread, and of course, the star of the show, his famous filet mignon! By using only olive oil, salt, and pepper, the flavor of the meat really shines. As you can imagine, these business lunches were a hit!

SERVES 4

4 (8-ounce) thick-cut filet mignons
4 teaspoons flaked kosher salt
2 teaspoons coarse ground black pepper
¼ cup extra-virgin olive oil

1 Set the Traeger grill to 225°F degrees and put a cast-iron skillet on the grill (to be used for searing). Cover the grill and preheat 15 minutes. Place the filets on a baking sheet and dry with a paper towel.

2 Sprinkle olive oil on the filet, followed by salt and pepper. Use your hands to massage the seasonings into the meat, making sure every inch is covered with flavor. Place the filets directly on grill grates and cook until the internal temperature reaches 130°F for medium-rare (or see chart, page 111, for desired doneness).

3 Put a cast-iron skillet on the grill while the steaks are cooking so it can begin to come to temperature. Transfer the filets to a platter and cover with foil. Turn the grill up as high as it gets. Once the grill is up to temp, place all four filets in the hot cast-iron skillet and sear for 1 to 2 minutes, turning once, or until desired crust is achieved. Let rest for 5 to 10 minutes before serving.

tip The quality of the filet mignon makes a big difference. We like to shop from a local butcher, but Costco has high-quality filets at good prices. If you want to go crazy, Snake River Farms has the best filets money can buy. To make the meat go further and for your guests to find their desired level of doneness, you can slice steak into ½-inch-thick slices before serving. For this recipe, turn on Super Smoke to get more flavor. 🥄

Fancy Grilled Lobster Tails

Our family hails from Long Island, New York, through San Francisco, so we love seafood. However, it wasn't until one of David's closest friends, our cousin Will, began diving off the coast of California, discovered a cavernous section of underwater terrain, and began supplying us with fresh lobster, that this recipe gained rock-star status. Now, Will fishes in the morning, and by afternoon, is grilling lobster for dinner. With a big family, lobster at home can be a fun way to celebrate a special occasion, or to serve as surf and turf for a seafood extravaganza!

SERVES 6

6 (8- to 10-ounce) lobster tails
½ cup (1 stick) unsalted butter
2 tablespoons lemon juice
1 teaspoon paprika

¼ teaspoon garlic salt
¼ teaspoon Old Bay seasoning
¼ teaspoon ground black pepper
2 tablespoons chopped fresh parsley

1   Set the Traeger grill to 400°F and preheat for 15 minutes with the lid closed.

2   Use kitchen shears to cut a slit lengthwise down the top and bottom of each lobster shell toward the tail. Using your fingers, gently pry the meat from the shell, keeping it attached at the base of the tail. Lift the meat so it rests atop the split shell (again, keeping it attached at the base of the tail). Use a paring knife to cut a slit down the middle of the lobster meat to butterfly it open. Place the lobster tails on a rimmed baking sheet.

3   Melt the butter in a small saucepan over medium-low heat. Whisk in the lemon juice, paprika, garlic salt, Old Bay, pepper, and parsley. Pour about 1 tablespoon of the butter mixture over each lobster tail. Keep the remaining butter mixture warm.

4   Set the lobster tails directly on the grill grates. Cook with the lid closed until the meat is white and opaque, 25 to 30 minutes. Transfer the lobster tails to a platter and serve with the remaining butter mixture.

Zesty Sriracha and Lime Salmon

This salmon dish is a family favorite for good reason. After Kristin had her twins, a friend brought over a flavorful spicy salmon dish. Kristin loved it so much, she decided to create her own Sriracha version. Marinated in a spicy-zesty sauce featuring Sriracha with lime, then roasted on the Traeger until it melts in your mouth, this salmon is a star on its own. Save some extra sauce for basting just prior to serving, then top with chopped cilantro.

SERVES 4

Grated zest and juice of **3** limes
4 tablespoons maple syrup
3 tablespoons Sriracha

1 teaspoon coarse sea salt
1 (2-pound) salmon fillet, skin removed
1 bunch fresh cilantro, coarsely chopped

1 Set the Traeger grill to 425°F and preheat with the lid closed for 15 minutes, or preheat the oven to 425°F.

2 In a bowl, whisk together the zest and juice, syrup, Sriracha, and salt. Place the salmon in a baking dish. (If the salmon is too long for the dish, either fold the fillet over at the narrower thin end or cut the narrow end off and place next to the salmon in the baking dish.) Pour one-third of the marinade over the salmon and marinate for 15 to 20 minutes.

3 Place the salmon on the grill grate and cook for 15 to 20 minutes, until the salmon is cooked through and flaky. Top with remaining sauce and sprinkle with cilantro. (If using the oven, use all of the marinade at the beginning, then roast until cooked through and flaky, about 15 minutes.)

Jeremy's Brisket Tips

Jeremy is so commonly known as Mr. Meats that it's hard to believe he hasn't always been a grill master, and in fact was once far more of a "functional eater," than a "foodie"! But shortly after buying Traeger Grills, Jeremy decided that he wanted to learn how to grill meat and grill it well. Not only did he want to better understand his business, but he also wanted to be able to feed all of the people he and Kristin were constantly inviting over! After years of practice, and guided by the expertise of Traeger's brilliant chefs, Jeremy developed his own method for smoking the perfect brisket. Jeremy's meticulously assembled recipe, accompanied by the best tips, is your guide to mastering the hardest cut of meat and the holy grail of barbecue!

HOW TO SELECT THE RIGHT BRISKET

Selecting the right brisket is an important part of creating something great! Look for lots of marbling, which leads to tenderness and flavor. A firm texture and a thick, even fat cap will help ensure your end result is juicy. Opt for Choice or Prime grades for top-quality meat, as they are recognized for their superior quality in grocery stores and butcher shops. Costco offers good value and high quality on brisket, but if you want to up your game, go to a local butcher and ask them to order the highest quality brisket. (Snake River Farms is our favorite splurge!) It's recommended to get a full packer, which includes both the point and the flat.

TRIM THE BRISKET

Trimming a brisket takes some instruction and practice. You can always ask the butcher to trim it, but developing brisket trimming expertise is part of the art and will help you feel like you've mastered the entire process. There are endless brisket trimming videos online. Jeremy recommends finding one on YouTube by Matt Pittman, founder of Meat Church. In short:

- Get rid of the "hard fat" that isn't going to render during the smoking process.

- Remove the fat and silverskin membrane on top that prevents direct seasoning of the meat. Leave about a ¼-inch fat layer on the bottom of the brisket

- Eliminate any edge of the meat that could make the finished product look less attractive.

- *Pro tip:* The colder the brisket, the easier it is to trim!

SEASON IT

Flavor is personal, so enjoy experimenting with different ways of seasoning your brisket. Jeremy likes to use a traditional base of kosher salt and ground pepper, which he applies to the entire surface area of the brisket. Adding equal amounts of Traeger Prime Rib Rub and Traeger Coffee Rub will enhance flavor and improve the quality of the brisket's texture and color of the bark.

SMOKE IT

Fill your hopper with your favorite brisket pellet flavor. Whichever flavor or blend you choose, hours of smoke rolling over your uncovered brisket will create a great flavor. For a more pronounced flavor profile, use a mesquite wood flavor, which is native to Texas. Then follow these steps:

- Set temperature of grill to 225°F. To enhance flavor, Jeremy recommends using the Super Smoke function on your Traeger grill if you have it.

- Place the brisket directly on the grill grate with the fat side down. This protects the meat because the fat absorbs the radiant heat.

- Cook brisket until internal temperature is around 165°F. If you have a Wi-Fi–connected Traeger and use a meat probe (both highly recommended), set your Traeger app to notify you when the brisket has reached this temperature. (Pro tip: Jeremy often puts his brisket on late at night as he hates the stress of it not being done on time. For a slightly longer cook, he sets the grill temp a bit lower to 200 °F and wraps it early in the morning). **Note:** A 15-pound brisket will take 10 to 12 hours to cook.

• Once your brisket has reached 165°F internal temperature, wrap it with either butcher paper or aluminum foil. (Measure the brisket temperature at the center portion of the area between the point and the flat of the brisket.)

• Jeremy likes to place his brisket in a disposable aluminum catering pan with about a ¼-inch of beef broth on the bottom of the pan. He then places foil over the pan.

• The finished temperature of a brisket will vary. That's the challenge of brisket— every cut is a bit different! An appropriate internal temperature is 203°F, but start to test for doneness around 198°F. You should feel little or no pressure when you insert a probe into the area where the flat meets the point of your brisket—a bit like putting a probe into room temperature butter. (Until you've practiced enough to recognize the tension of inserting a probe, feel confident in taking it off at 203°F).

LET IT REST AND THEN SLICE AWAY!

• A brisket should rest after cooking for at least 30 minutes before serving. As a brisket rests, all of those delicious juices can settle down and redistribute. Longer is better, and resting for 3 hours or more will create the best texture.

• A long rest also provides flexibility around when you eat. When resting a brisket for longer than an hour, it's good practice to transfer the brisket to an insulated cooler to keep the brisket in a safe temperature zone as it rests. Burp the brisket by lifting the foil for 15 seconds when pulling it off the Traeger and then again after each hour until serving. When using butcher paper, overwrap the resting brisket with plastic wrap, then wrap in a towel prior to placing in an insulated cooler.

• Always slice brisket against the grain for maximum juiciness. When you get toward the point, where the grain changes, rotate the brisket and cut thicker slices at the very end. Matt Pittman has good brisket-slicing advice on YouTube that will show you this process better than trying to describe it through writing in a cookbook!

• **Pro tip:** Save the au jus from the tin in which the brisket was cooking. Dip each slice prior to eating, or carefully poor over the top of your freshly sliced brisket!

• Jeremy likes to eat his brisket hot and without any sauce. That said, it's all a function of personal taste: some like to put different kinds of Traeger BBQ Sauces on brisket.

Jeremy's Brisket Recipe

SERVES 8

12–15 lb whole brisket, trimmed
Traeger Prime Rib Rub
Traeger Coffee Rub

Kosher salt
Ground pepper

1   Season your brisket liberally with kosher salt, ground pepper, and both Traeger rubs, then cover the brisket. Transfer the covered brisket to the refrigerator and let sit for 12 to 24 hours.

2   When ready to cook, choose your favorite Traeger pellets, set the Traeger temperature to 225°F, and preheat with the lid closed for 15 minutes. For optimal flavor, use Super Smoke, if available.

3   Unwrap the brisket. Insert the probe into the center portion of the area between the point and the flat of the brisket, then place directly on the grill grates, fat-side down. Close the lid and cook until internal temperature reaches 165°F, about 6 hours. Pro tip: put the brisket on the night before and wrap it in the morning to finish cooking. It's fine for the brisket to cook higher than 165°F unwrapped.

4   Remove the brisket from the grill and wrap in a double layer of heavy-duty aluminum foil or butcher paper or put in an aluminum catering tin with a quarter inch beef broth and some beef tallow on top, and cover with aluminum foil.

5   Place the wrapped brisket back on the grill and cook until the internal temperature reaches 203°F, approximately 3 to 4 hours more.

6   Remove the brisket from the grill and let rest in the foil for at least 30 minutes. Unwrap and slice against the grain. Enjoy!

Leftover Brisket is the Best!
You can reheat your brisket, covered with foil, on the Traeger at 350°F for 20 to 30 minutes and enjoy as-is or use leftovers for brisket tacos, hash, or omelets!

Smoked Citrus Salt

Our family loves salt—from Himalayan pink salt to Maldon sea salt flakes. So, naturally, as we were gathering our recipes for this cookbook, we decided that we should create our very own! This Smoked Citrus Salt is a celebration of our favorite flavors in a single sprinkle!

---

1 cup flaky kosher salt
1 teaspoon dried parsley
1 teaspoon dried cilantro
1 teaspoon smoked paprika
Zest of one lime, one orange, and one lemon

1   Set the Traeger grill to 225°F. Cover and preheat for 15 minutes.

2   Spread out one cup flaky kosher salt on a 13x18-inch sheet pan.

3   Add 1 teaspoon of parsley, cilantro, and smoked paprika to the kosher salt.

4   Using a zester, zest one lime, one orange, and one lemon on top of the salt. Mix.

5   Smoke the salt on a Traeger for 40 minutes, ensuring that your zest does not get burnt or too dark brown. You want it to be a light, amber brown when it is done.

6   Remove from oven and let cool. Store salt in an airtight container up to 3 weeks or in the refrigerator for 2 to 3 months.

I'D SMOKE THAT!
OUR FAVORITE TRAEGER'D ADDITIONS

If the Andrus family is not hosting people on a Sunday night, there is an outcry among the children. The truth is, the week just doesn't feel complete without a moment spent gathering around the wood-fired grill! The Andrus children are also always requesting new foods to Traeger. While we can't say all foods taste better on the Traeger, we haven't found a food that doesn't! Practically speaking, when the Traeger is already fired up and hot, we love to add to it, whether it's with our sides, dessert, or even something to serve the next night. Not only does the smoky infusion enhance the flavor of basic leftovers, but the Traeger also transforms even basic takeout into a moment to gather!

Follow all basic preparation and oven directions for any of the following. Then put on the Traeger grill instead of in the oven:

- Popcorn and caramel popcorn
- Homemade Chex mix
- Frozen lasagna
- Take-and-bake pizza
- Pre-made macaroni and cheese
- Frozen meals or appetizers
- Pizookie
- Brownies
- Butter
- Leftovers
- Homemade salts
- Bread
- Pillsbury crescent rolls

CHAPTER 5

Side Hustle

One thing we've learned after years of grilling and smoking is to never neglect the sides! The variety of colors, textures, and flavors available is not only endless, but the right side complements a heavy dish, countering savory with sweet, and vice-versa. For example, we love pairing our juicy **Pork Tenderloin with Citrus Chimichurri Sauce (see page 125)** with our delicious **Asian Citrus Slaw (see page 152)**; and we hardly ever make our **Smoky Reverse-Seared Tri-Tip (see page 123)** without a side of our **Crispy Smashed Potatoes (see page 146)**.

Our family's favorite way to spruce up a simple vegetable side, such as asparagus, green beans, or sweet potatoes, is with our go-to **Easy Veggie Marinade (see page 162)**. We often make large batches of our **Everyday Roasted Sheet-Pan Veggies (see page 161)** and add leftovers to breakfast (see our **Kitchen Sink Breakfast Hash (page 37)**) or salads.

Tiffany, a professional dance instructor, and her husband Matthew, a professional stuntman, are our family's most health-conscious duo and are constantly experimenting with new ways to eat vegetables. Our **Coconut Curry Cauliflower (see page 143)** is a great meat replacement and can be served over rice to complete a meal. However, despite a focus on keeping their lean physiques, even they agree that some recipes are simply too good to leave the rotation, such as Matt's delicious **Skillet Cornbread (see page 159)**.

The great thing about sides is they don't have to be complicated. Not only can they act as vegetarian substitutes, but they also tend to make the food go farther. We love to bring a vegetable dish to contribute to a party or event, and we often ask friends to bring sides to our own gatherings—it's a great way to invite friends to participate and feel included! Whether a side is indulgent, like our **Grilled Cheesy Pull-Apart Bread (see page 151)**, or nostalgic, like our **Comfort Creamy Corn Pudding (see page 154)**, we recommend incorporating one next time you fire up the Traeger!

Coconut Curry Cauliflower

This recipe proves that vegetables are not boring! An exotic combination of curry and paprika, balanced with currants and toasted coconut, is sure to please even your pickiest vegetable eater. This dish goes with almost everything, and we love how the unique flavors will surprise and delight your guests or family. This is also a great go-to main course option for any vegetarian eaters out there and can be made a complete meal when served with sticky rice or cooked quinoa.

SERVES 8–10

Cauliflower Curry Sauce
¾ **cup** extra-virgin olive oil
½ **cup** red wine vinegar
2 **cloves** garlic, minced
1 **tablespoon** cumin
1 **tablespoon** curry powder
1 **teaspoon** paprika
½ **teaspoon** salt
¼ **teaspoon** ground black pepper

1½ **heads** cauliflower, cut or broken into bite-size pieces
1 **cup** sweetened coconut flakes
1 purple onion, chopped
⅔ **cup** currants, golden raisins, or pomegranate seeds
½ **cup** chopped fresh parsley

1 Preheat the oven to 400°F.

2 *For the sauce:* In a small bowl, mix together all the ingredients.

3 Put the cauliflower, onion, and ½ cup of the coconut flakes into a larger bowl, pour the sauce over it, and mix.

4 Spread the mixture on a baking sheet and roast for 15 minutes, until golden brown.

5 Remove from the oven, add the remaining ½ cup coconut, the currants and raisins, and the parsley, and serve.

Southern Collard Greens

Tiffany's husband, Matthew, grew up in the South, where knowing how to cook collard greens is a requirement, and his grandmother's recipe was the best! So of course, when Tiffany joined the Simmons family, she had to learn how to make it too! Although she's updated it and simplified a few steps, these collard greens are a staple in their home.

SERVES 12

2 ham hocks

2 (2-pound) bags chopped collard greens

4 cups chicken stock

½ cup chopped onion

2 tablespoons granulated sugar

2 tablespoons unsalted butter

2 tablespoons Worcestershire sauce

2 tablespoons apple cider vinegar

1 tablespoon crushed red pepper flakes

½ teaspoon garlic powder

¼ teaspoon paprika

1 tablespoon salt

1   Place the ham hocks in a large pot and add enough water to submerge the hocks. Cover and cook over medium heat for 45 minutes.

2   Add the greens, chicken stock, and all the remaining ingredients to the pot. Cover and cook for 2 hours. Then remove lid and cook for an additional hour, or until the greens are completely tender. Most of the water should have evaporated by this point, just leaving enough to cover the greens.

3   Fish out the ham hocks and remove the meat from the bones. Discard the fat, skin, and bones. Chop the meat, stir back into the greens, and serve the collards.

Crispy Smashed Potatoes

These smashed potatoes are like a cheesy baked French fry that packs a punch of flavor in every bite. Red potatoes are baked, then smashed and roasted with extra seasoning, and finished with cheese for the ultimate comfort side dish. They pair well with any protein and vegetable. We love making lots of these and using the leftovers the next day served with leftover protein and sour cream.

SERVES 8

16 small red potatoes
⅓ **cup** plus ½ **cup** extra-virgin olive oil
1 **tablespoon** chopped fresh rosemary
2 **teaspoons** salt

1 **teaspoon** ground black pepper
1 **cup** shredded Parmesan, feta, or cheddar cheese, optional

1   Set the Traeger grill to 350°F and preheat with the lid closed for 15 minutes (or preheat the oven).

2   Place the potatoes directly on the grill grate or oven rack and cook for 30 minutes, or until a fork easily inserts. Lay the potatoes on a rimmed baking sheet to cool for 5 to 10 minutes. Turn the oven or Traeger up to 400°F.

3   Drizzle the potatoes with ⅓ cup olive oil. Crush each potato with a spatula until smashed down but still intact. Drizzle the ½ cup olive oil on top of the smashed potatoes, or use more if you want crispier potatoes. Sprinkle with the rosemary, salt, and pepper.

4   Place the baking sheet on the grill or in the oven and cook the smashed potatoes for 15 minutes, or until crispy. Top with cheese for the last 5 minutes of baking, if you like.

tip Don't crowd the baking sheet—leave space between each potato or they won't crisp.

Sweet Potato and Carrot Mash

For over fifty years, Laurie and her friend Christine have been sharing recipes. Even now, they are discovering and developing new twists on old classics. Our family loves sweet potatoes, whether baked as a side or roasted to top salads. So, when Christine recently shared this recipe, it became an instant hit! The combination of sweet potato and carrot, combined with crème fraîche and nutmeg, is the ultimate fall treat.

SERVES 6

4 large sweet potatoes or yams

1 pound carrots, peeled, trimmed, and cut into 5-inch lengths

2½ cups water

1 tablespoon granulated sugar

12 tablespoons (1½ sticks) unsalted butter, softened

Salt & ground black pepper, to taste

½ cup crème fraîche

½ teaspoon ground nutmeg

Dash of cayenne pepper, optional

1   Preheat the oven to 375°F. Scrub the sweet potatoes and cut a small deep slit in the top of each.

2   Set the potatoes on the center rack of the oven and bake for 1 hour, or until tender when pierced with a fork.

3   Meanwhile, in a saucepan, combine the carrots, water, sugar, 2 tablespoons of the butter, and salt and pepper to taste. Bring to a boil over medium heat and cook uncovered until water has evaporated and carrots begin to sizzle in the butter, about 30 minutes. The carrots should be tender; if not, add a little water and cook until tender and the liquid has evaporated.

4   Scrape the flesh from the sweet potatoes into the bowl of a food processor. Add the carrots, remaining 10 tablespoons butter, and the crème fraîche and process until very smooth. Add the nutmeg, season with salt and pepper, and cayenne if desired. Remove from food processor and place in serving dish.

Grilled Cheesy Pull-Apart Bread

We didn't think our favorite food—bread with butter and salt—could be improved upon, but the Traeger team did so in creating this riff on a bloomin' onion! With your bread loaf cut open into a blossom, drizzled with melted butter, slathered with pesto, and stuffed with cheese, you have the ultimate finger food side dish that will pair well with any protein dish, pasta bake, and more!

SERVES 12

1 sourdough round or loaf, or rustic
   French or Italian loaf
½ **cup (1 stick)** unsalted butter, melted
1 **cup** prepared pesto
1½ **cups** shredded Italian-style cheese blend

1 Set the Traeger grill to 350°F and preheat for 15 minutes with the lid closed (or preheat the oven).

2 Using a bread knife, slice the bread in about 1½-inch-wide rows in one direction, but leaving the bottom 1 inch intact. Rotate the bread 90 degrees and cut in the other direction, creating cube shapes attached to the bottom of the loaf. Use your fingers to widen the bread.

3 Place the bread on a sheet of foil large enough to wrap around the entire loaf. Pour the melted butter into the bread cuts. Using a spoon, spread the pesto into the cuts, then stuff the cuts with the cheese. Fold up the edges of the foil and wrap the loaf to enclose, then transfer to a baking sheet.

4 Place the baking sheet directly on the grill grate or on the rack in the oven. Cook for 15 minutes, then unwrap the foil. Cook for 5 to 10 minutes longer, until the cheese is melted. Remove from the foil and serve.

Asian Citrus Slaw

Asian Citrus Slaw is an adaptable, healthy way to get in your veggies and freshen up any meal. We add it to leftover salmon to make fish tacos or serve it alongside any protein as a light salad. With six active children and a husband who loves grilling delicious meats, Kristin often serves protein bowls for quick, assemble-yourself, weeknight dinners. Having leftover lean protein in the fridge from the weekend and a large batch of this slaw marinating in the fridge makes it easy to throw together a healthy and filling dinner that everybody loves!

SERVES 12

1 **(12-ounce) bag** broccoli slaw or 1 head
   purple cabbage, sliced

1 **(10-ounce) bag** shredded carrots

1 **bunch** scallions, sliced

½ red bell pepper, seeded and diced

½ **bunch** fresh cilantro, roughly
   chopped, some reserved for garnish

½ **cup** lime juice

2 **tablespoons** sesame oil

2 **tablespoons** soy sauce

2 **tablespoons** sugar

1 **dash** of Sriracha

1 **tablespoon** sesame seeds

Chopped peanuts or cashews, optional

1   In a large bowl, combine the slaw mix, carrots, scallions, bell pepper, and cilantro. In a small bowl, combine the lime juice, sesame oil, soy sauce, sugar, and Sriracha and whisk until the sugar is dissolved.

2   Pour the sauce over the slaw mix and combine until all the slaw is coated. Just before serving, top with additional cilantro, sesame seeds, and peanuts, if you like. Store in the fridge for up to 5 days.

tip To save on time, we often use pre-shredded gourmet slaw mixes: Brussel sprout slaw, broccoli slaw, carrot slaw...they all work! ✎

Comfort Creamy Corn Pudding

Laurie was visiting her local hardware store in California when she saw the orange "Traeger Tent." Although the meat wasn't finished smoking, the corn pudding was hot, bubbly, and ready for sampling! After tasting this ultimate comfort food creation, Laurie was so impressed, she asked for the recipe card and took it home with her. Cooked in a cast-iron skillet, this savory pudding is one of those "worth it" dishes. While it's true we try to choose lean proteins, veggies, and complex carbs for dinner, this warm and comforting dish takes any meal to the next level!

SERVES 12

1 **(15-ounce) can** creamed-style corn

1 **(15-ounce) can** golden sweet corn, drained, or **1 (16-ounce) bag** frozen corn, thawed

1 **(8-ounce) package** Jiffy corn muffin mix

1 **(8-ounce) package** cream cheese, diced small

1 **(8-ounce) package** shredded cheddar cheese

1 **(8-ounce) container** sour cream

½ **cup** buttermilk

4 **tablespoons (½ stick)** salted butter, diced

2 extra-large eggs (or **3** medium eggs)

1½ **teaspoons** salt

½ **teaspoon** ground black pepper

1   Set the Traeger grill to 375°F or preheat the oven. Spray a Dutch oven, 9x13-inch casserole dish, or ovenproof large cast-iron skillet, with nonstick cooking oil.

2   In a large mixing bowl, stir all ingredients together until combined. Pour the batter into the baking dish and cover with a lid or foil. Place on the grill grate or in the oven and cook the corn pudding for 1 hour.

3   Remove the lid or foil, carefully stir the pudding, then cook covered for an additional 30 minutes, or until golden brown. Let rest for 10 minutes before serving.

Salt-Crusted Baked Potatoes

Bring on the salt with these salt-crusted baked potatoes! They are the number one side dish requested by our kids. The potato centers are fluffy and soft, while the skins are perfectly crunchy and salty. We love serving these with all the toppings: sour cream, shredded cheese, bacon bits, chives—you name it!

SERVES 8

8 large russet potatoes
¾ **cup** extra-virgin olive oil
1 **cup** flaked kosher or sea salt

1   Set the Traeger grill to 350°F. Cover and preheat for 15 minutes. If you make these in the oven, follow the same directions.

2   Scrub, wash, and dry potatoes. Poke each potato with a fork 2 or 3 times. Set the potatoes on a baking sheet and rub olive oil over each, making sure all surface area is covered. Sprinkle liberally with salt, ensuring all surface area is covered.

3   Put potatoes directly on the grill grate and cook for 1 hour, or until a fork easily inserts into the potato. Remove from heat and serve, topping them with all your favorite fixings.

tip Meat thermometers work great with baked potatoes. You know they are done when the middle of the potato registers at 205°F. We always make extra potatoes so we can have potato skins the next day: Slice them in half and top with chili, cheese, or leftovers and broil.

Skillet Cornbread

Cornbread is a staple on most Southern dinner tables, so it's been a favorite of Matthew's for a long time! This version, inspired by Banderas restaurant in Corona Del Mar, has been perfected over two decades and has become one of our most requested sides. It's not only easy to make, but also easily complements pretty much any meat you have already smoking on the Traeger! It freezes well and leftovers—if you happen to have them!—can be made into **Cornbread Croutons (page 84)**.

SERVES 16

1 **cup (2 sticks)** salted butter, melted
1 **cup** granulated sugar
4 large eggs
1 **(15-ounce) can** creamed-style corn
1 **(4-ounce) can** chopped green chile peppers, drained
½ **cup** shredded Monterey jack cheese

½ **cup** shredded cheddar cheese
1 **cup** all-purpose flour
1 **cup** yellow cornmeal
4 **teaspoons** baking powder
1 **teaspoon** salt
Butter and honey, for serving

1   Preheat the oven to 300°F and lightly grease a 12-inch cast-iron skillet.

2   In a large bowl, beat together the butter and sugar. Beat in the eggs one at a time. Blend in the creamed corn, chiles, Monterey jack, and cheddar. In a separate bowl, stir together the flour, cornmeal, baking powder, and salt. Add the flour mixture to the corn mixture and stir just until smooth.

3   Pour the batter into the prepared skillet and bake for 1 hour, until a wooden pick inserted into the center of the pan comes out clean. Slice into wedges and top with butter and honey.

Everyday Roasted Sheet-Pan Veggies

Here's a recipe we cook at least twice a week! It's foolproof and gets the entire family to eat their veggies! Just keep in mind that the cooking should be fast and hot, not slow and low. We mix and match the vegetables and haven't found any combination that doesn't work. For a normal weeknight dinner, you can skip the parsley, but it sure is a pretty touch for entertaining. The perfect shortcut for this recipe is using Trader Joe's pre-cut onions and frozen garlic cubes for the marinade.

SERVES 8

4 **cups** diced butternut squash or sweet potatoes

1 **head** broccoli or cauliflower, cut or broken into pieces

2 **cups** sliced mushrooms

1 chopped onion

1½ **cups** Easy Everyday Veggie Marinade (see page 162)

¼ **cup** chopped fresh flat-leaf parsley, optional

1   Set the Traeger grill to 375°F and preheat for 15 minutes with the lid closed (or preheat the oven).

2   Prepare the **Easy Everyday Veggie Marinade** (see page 162).

3   In a large bowl, combine the squash, broccoli, mushrooms, and onion. Drizzle with the marinade, while continuing to mix the marinade to ensure you get garlic and balsamic over everything. Toss everything with your hands until the vegetables are evenly coated. Spread the vegetables in an even layer on 1 or 2 baking sheets, ensuring there is a bit of space between each piece. (If the vegetables are too crowded, they will steam instead of roast and you won't get that crispy texture.)

4   Place the baking sheet(s) on the grill grate or in the oven and cook for 15 minutes. Stir, then continue to cook until the vegetables are browned around the edges, 5 to 10 minutes longer.

5   Garnish the vegetables with the parsley, then serve immediately or at room temperature. Enjoy!

Easy Everyday Veggie Marinade

Get your kids eating more veggies with this easy veggie marinade!

MAKES 1¹/₂ CUPS

1 cup extra-virgin olive oil
⅓ cup balsamic glaze (not balsamic vinegar)
4 garlic cloves, minced
1 tablespoon kosher salt
1 tablespoon cracked black pepper

In a small bowl, whisk together all the ingredients. Use with your favorite vegetables. Make extra to keep on hand; it'll keep in the fridge for 3 to 5 days.

Other Sheet-Pan Possibilities: Our sheet-pan recipe is infinitely adaptable. Try the combinations below or start mixing and matching with what you have in the fridge. Note that the roasting times may be longer or shorter, depending on the density and amount of vegetables. Here are some of our favorite flavor combinations!

Sheet-Pan Broccoli or Broccolini
Broccoli or broccolini
Extra-virgin olive oil
Lemon zest or juice
Minced garlic
Sliced shallots
Salt or garlic salt
Ground black pepper

Sheet-Pan Green Beans
Sesame oil
Soy sauce
Sugar
Sesame seeds

Sheet-Pan Butternut Squash
Extra-virgin olive oil
Brown sugar
Maple syrup
Cinnamon
Cayenne pepper
Salt

CHAPTER 6

Throwbacks

Grandma Ruth always said that eating lentils on New Year's Day would bring good luck and prosperity. Our family has embraced this heartwarming tradition; we've always eaten **Ruth's Hearty Lentil Soup (see page 185)** on New Year's Day, and we are indeed, abundantly blessed! When you have good food and good friends, there is so much to be grateful for!

Although our family prioritizes healthy meals, we all love to indulge in some of these beloved throwback recipes that transport us back to our idyllic childhood in Walnut Creek. From poolside chats over **Kathy's Snoopy Seafood Pasta Salad (see page 169)** to dinner conversations over **Laurie's Triple-Layer Lasagna (see page 172)**, each dish is attached to a person, a memory, or a tradition—that's one of our favorite things about documenting these passed-down recipes!

Over the years, we have also added our own comfort food favorites to this list. When Tiffany merged her love of veggies with a craving for Thai food, she created a once-new, now-old family favorite: **Tiffany's Thai Vegetable Soup (see page 179)**. And when Miriam introduced us to her family's recipe, we all added **Miriam's Brazilian Beef Stroganoff (see page 182)** to our dinner repertoire!

Additionally, many of these recipes are also ideal for feeding a large group. Mom learned from Grandma Ruth—who would make five gallons of soup for guests!—how far a large pot of soup can go. Now, whenever anyone comes to town, Mom is known to whip up a huge pot of **Christine's Classic Minestrone Soup (see page 171)**.

Us Moore siblings treasure our shared memories of spending time at Grandma Dot's condo, and running around the grass in her big backyard before Sunday dinner. These throwback recipes evoke those same nostalgic feelings of being with family and friends while embracing the lovely atmosphere around us. How blessed we are!

Kristin's Healthy White Bean and Chicken Chili

This recipe has won more contests than we can count, including Trunk-or-Treats and even a Traeger Chili Cook-Off! It's rare to find comfort food that's also healthy. Yet this recipe, with lean protein, veggies, and flavorful spices, is both! We also love this the next day over baked potatoes or as a dip.

SERVES 8–10

2 **tablespoons** olive oil

3 **medium** yellow onions, chopped

4 **cloves** garlic, minced, or 4 Trader Joe's frozen garlic cubes

2 bell peppers, seeded and chopped

2 **(16-ounce) packages** ground chicken (0 to 7% fat)

2 **tablespoons** chili powder

1 **tablespoon** Mexican seasoning

1 **tablespoon** cumin

1½ **teaspoons** paprika

Salt & ground black pepper, to taste

1 **(8-ounce) container** sliced mushrooms

3 **(4-ounce) cans** green chiles

1 **(12-ounce) bag** frozen corn

4 **(15-ounce) cans** white beans, drained

2 **(32-ounce) cartons** chicken stock

Cayenne pepper

Optional toppings

sour cream, cubed avocado, **Cornbread Croutons (page 84)**, chopped cilantro, sliced scallions, sliced jalapeños

1   Heat the oil in a large pot over medium heat. Add the onions, garlic, and bell peppers and cook until softened. Add the ground chicken and stir until the chicken is cooked through and beginning to brown, about 5 to 8 minutes.

2   Stir in the chili powder, Mexican seasoning, cumin, paprika, and salt and pepper and mix into the chicken. Add the mushrooms, green chiles, corn, and beans and cook until the mixture is warmed through. Add 1 carton of the chicken stock. Taste and add more seasoning as needed, plus a little cayenne for a kick. Simmer for 1 to 3 hours (or as long as you can). Halfway through simmering, add the remaining carton of stock if the liquid has evaporated considerably. You can also smoke the chili in an oven-safe pot on the Traeger at 300°F for 2 hours. Finish off your chili with your toppings of choice and serve.

Kathy's Snoopy Seafood Salad

For years, Kristin and Danielle were heavily involved in synchronized swimming. Besides international and transcontinental travel, we often had local competitive meets. This meant we needed nutritious, delicious food to feed all of the girls and their moms during the long hours on deck. A family friend, Kathy, made this for us once, and it became a favorite! Now when we eat this salad, we look back fondly on those years spent at the pool!

SERVES 8

1 pound medium cooked shrimp
  (save a few for garnish)
1 bunch scallions, finely chopped
1½ cups chopped celery
Salt & lemon pepper, to taste
½ cup Italian salad dressing
8 to 10 ounces capellini or
  spaghetti pasta

¾ cup mayonnaise
¼ cup fresh lemon juice
½ cup grated Parmesan cheese, plus
  more for garnish
Toppings
  cooked shrimp, black or green olives,
  halved cherry tomatoes, hard-boiled
  eggs, sliced avocado

1   In a large bowl, combine the shrimp, scallions, celery, salt, and lemon pepper. Add the Italian dressing, cover, and set aside to marinate for 30 minutes.

2   Meanwhile, cook the pasta in salted boiling water with a dollop of oil according to package directions until al dente. Rinse with cold water.

3   Add the noodles to the shrimp mixture, along with the mayonnaise, lemon juice, and Parmesan cheese, and toss to mix. Cover and refrigerate for up to 48 hours (it's best if made the day before serving).

4   Serve the salad on a platter, garnished with additional Parmesan cheese, shrimp, olives, tomatoes, hard-boiled egg slices, and avocado.

Christine's Classic Minestrone Soup

This tasty minestrone soup is one of the many recipes our mom copied from her friend Christine's recipe box in 1973. Even years later, our mom and Christine are still great friends, and this minestrone soup is still one of our family's favorite soup recipes. It's healthy, packed with vegetables, and is a filling entrée to have with rolls, a salad, or alongside grilled cheese.

SERVES 12

2 **tablespoons** extra-virgin olive oil
1 onion, chopped
2 **cloves** garlic, minced, or **2 cubes** Trader Joe's frozen garlic
3 **tablespoons** Better than Bouillon beef base
1 **(28-ounce) jar** marinara sauce
6 **cups** water
1 **(10-ounce) bag** shredded carrots
1 **to 2 cups** chopped celery
2 **(10-ounce) bags** chopped green cabbage
3 large zucchini, sliced
1 **(15-ounce) can** kidney beans, drained
1 **(13-ounce) package** turkey kielbasa, sliced and sautéed
3 **cups** fresh spinach or baby kale
2 **cups** cooked small pasta shells
2 **teaspoons** salt
½ **teaspoon** ground black pepper
Grated Parmesan cheese, for serving

1   Heat the olive oil in a large skillet over medium heat. Add the onion and garlic and sauté until softened. Add the beef bouillon, marinara, water, carrots, celery, and cabbage. Cook until all the vegetables are tender, about 10 minutes.

2   Add the zucchini, kidney beans, and kielbasa and cook until the zucchini is softened, about 4 to 6 minutes. Add the fresh spinach or kale and cook just until wilted, about 2 minutes. Let the soup cool slightly, then stir in the cooked pasta. Season with salt and pepper and serve with Parmesan cheese.

Laurie's Triple-Layer Lasagna

This recipe was inspired by the recipe in the red-and-white-checked Better Homes and Garden cookbook binder (remember those?!). Mom made it for us when we were growing up, and it was the first recipe Kristin ever made Jeremy. Twenty years later, Kristin is still making it! Layers of noodles, cheese, and rustic sauce is the perfect combination. The middle gets saucy and creamy while the top has a crispy, cheesy layer, thanks to heaping spoonfuls of Parmesan. It's easy to make ahead of time and is only better when served as leftovers.

SERVES 8

2 tablespoons olive oil

1½ onions, chopped

3 cloves garlic, minced

1 pound ground meat (extra lean beef, chicken, or turkey all work great)

1 (8-ounce) package sliced mushrooms

1 can fire roasted, diced tomatoes

3 (24-ounce) bottles of your favorite pasta sauce (I love Rao's brand; whatever you use, make sure it's pretty soupy so that you have moist lasagna)

1 (16-ounce) container ricotta cheese

5 cups shredded mozzarella cheese

1 cup grated Parmesan cheese

1 (12-ounce) package frozen spinach, thawed and drained

2 medium eggs

1 teaspoon dried basil

1 teaspoon dried oregano

1 teaspoon salt

½ teaspoon ground black pepper

1 (9-ounce) package oven-ready lasagna noodles (you may not use the whole package)

1   Preheat the oven to 350°F.

2   In a medium saucepan, heat the oil over medium heat. Add the onions and cook until translucent, about 8 to 10 minutes. Add the garlic and cook until fragrant, about 2 to 3 minutes. Stir in the ground meat and cook until no pink remains. Add the canned tomatoes and mushrooms and bring everything to a simmer. Add pasta sauce and simmer for about 5 minutes or until thickened. Set the meat sauce aside.

3   In a large bowl, combine the ricotta, 1 cup of the mozzarella, the Parmesan, spinach, eggs, basil, oregano, salt, and pepper. Stir until mixed and set aside.

4 Now it's time to assemble everything! Start by layering 1 cup of the meat sauce on the bottom of a 9x13-inch glass baking dish, followed by 3 lasagna noodles, then ½ cup of ricotta cheese mixture, and 1 cup of the mozzarella cheese. Continue to layer, following a similar pattern, to make three layers, or until you've reached the top of the pan. Combine the remaining 1 cup mozzarella and Parmesan and sprinkle over the top.

5 Bake for 45 minutes. Check the middle to ensure it is cooked through. Cover the pan with foil and continue to bake for 15 to 20 more minutes, until the lasagna is toasty on top. Let it sit for at least 15 to 20 minutes before serving.

tip This recipe is perfect to make ahead of time, then pull out and bake when you're ready for dinner. We love adding in extra vegetables!

Dot's Broccoli Chicken Divan

When Grandpa Gunter passed away, Grandma Dot moved out to Walnut Creek, California, where our family was living. Although she had a small condo, she always invited the entire family over on Sundays for dinner. We would enjoy sharing family stories from over the years and especially looked forward to our beloved Uncle Scott stopping by to make us laugh! Chicken Divan was often on the menu. The creamy, cheesy sauce is the perfect complement to tender chicken and crunchy broccoli!

SERVES 6

4 to 5 cups fresh broccoli florets and thinly sliced stems, par-cooked in salted water and drained

1½ pounds cooked chicken breast meat (I use two large chicken breasts from a Costco rotisserie chicken)

1 (10.5-ounce) can cream of chicken soup

½ cup mayonnaise

¼ cup sour cream

1 teaspoon lemon juice

1 teaspoon curry powder

1½ to 2 cups shredded cheese (mozzarella, Monterey jack, or Colby)

1 cup French's crispy fried onions

1   Preheat the oven to 350°F. Generously butter the bottom of a 9x13-inch glass baking dish.

2   Place the par-cooked broccoli in the baking dish and top with the cooked chicken.

3   In a medium bowl, mix together the soup, mayonnaise, sour cream, lemon juice, and curry powder. Spread the mixture on top of the broccoli and chicken and top evenly with the cheese. Sprinkle with French's fried onions.

4   Cover with foil and bake for 25 to 30 minutes, removing the foil the last 5 to 10 minutes, until the cheese is melted and the fried onions are lightly toasted.

Tiffany's Thai Vegetable Soup

When Tiffany moved away from home to Los Angeles, she craved a healthy and delicious meal she could make once and eat several nights in a row. Her Thai Vegetable Soup, a fusion of Tom Kha Kai Soup and Panang Curry, has now become a staple in our family. Throughout the years, the recipe has been enhanced with lemongrass and ginger paste to ensure the soup is a little sweet, a little spicy, and a lot of flavor!

SERVES 8–12

1 **tablespoon** coconut oil

1 onion, chopped

1 **tablespoon** ginger paste (or fresh grated ginger)

2 **cloves** garlic, crushed

3 **tablespoons** red Thai curry paste

2 **tablespoons** lemongrass paste

4 **cups** chicken or vegetable stock

2 **(14-ounce) cans** coconut milk

2 **tablespoons** coconut sugar or regular sugar

1 **to** 2 **tablespoons** Sriracha, to taste

1 **tablespoon** soy sauce

1 large red bell pepper, seeded and chopped

4 **cups** chopped cauliflower

4 **cups** chopped broccoli

3 **cups** sliced yellow squash

2 **cups** sliced carrots

2 **cups** sliced mushrooms

¼ **cup** creamy peanut butter

3 **cups** chopped or shredded cooked chicken

3 **tablespoons** fresh squeezed lime juice

Chopped cilantro, for garnish

Cooked brown rice, for serving

1 In a large pot, heat the coconut oil over medium heat. Add the onion, ginger, garlic, curry paste, and lemongrass and stir-fry until the onion softens, 3 to 5 minutes. Add the stock, bring to a simmer, and simmer for 25 minutes.

2 Add the coconut milk, sugar, Sriracha, soy sauce, bell pepper, cauliflower, broccoli, squash, carrots, and mushrooms. Simmer for another 20 minutes, or until the vegetables are cooked through.

3 Stir in the peanut butter and add the cooked chicken. Remove from heat and add the lime juice. Garnish with chopped cilantro and serve with rice. (We add a large scoop of brown rice to each bowl and then ladle soup on.)

Nellie's Baked Stuffed Clams

Our dad grew up on the East Coast on Long Island, New York, where seafood was fresh and commonplace. There were a few dishes our grandma Ruth would make that we always remember, and baked stuffed clams was one of them! Now, Aunt Nellie and Tiffany have carried on the tradition. Chopped clams, bacon, and a breadcrumb mixture is stuffed into large clam shells and baked until crispy, rich, and delicious! They are a real "wow" factor for your dinner table or party spread and are so much fun to eat!

SERVES 24

5 (6.5-ounce) cans chopped clams, drained (reserve the clam broth)
2 pounds bacon, chopped
1 medium white onion, chopped
1 (15-ounce) package Italian seasoned breadcrumbs

1 teaspoon garlic powder
½ teaspoon salt
½ teaspoon ground black pepper
½ cup grated Parmesan cheese
2 dozen medium-sized clam shells
1 lemon, cut into wedges

1 Preheat the oven to 350°F. Evenly arrange the clam shells on a standard 9x13-inch baking sheet. In a food processor or blender, pulse the clams until finely chopped.

2 In a large frying pan over medium heat, cook the bacon until crispy. Transfer the bacon to a bowl with a slotted spoon, keeping the bacon fat in the pan. Add the onion to the pan and sauté for about 10 minutes, until softened.

3 Add the onion to the bacon in the bowl, along with the chopped clams. Stir in the breadcrumbs, garlic powder, salt, and pepper, then the Parmesan. Add half of the reserved clam juice to make the mixture moist.

4 Fill the clam shells with the stuffing. Bake for 30 minutes, or until browned on top. We serve the clams with lemon wedges and squeeze fresh lemon juice on top.

Miriam's Brazilian Beef Stroganoff

Our sister-in-law, Miriam, grew up in Brazil where "Estrogonofe de Carne" is a traditional meal for special occasions. This recipe is from Miriam's mother. They would enjoy this dish once a month when they had religious missionaries over for dinner. Be sure to top with shoestring potatoes for the ultimate Brazilian touch!

SERVES 8–10

About 4 tablespoons olive oil
3 pounds top sirloin, cut into strips, at room temperature
2 white onions, finely chopped
3 cloves garlic, finely chopped
3 tablespoons tomato paste

3 tablespoons ketchup
3 tablespoons Worcestershire sauce
2 cups sliced mushrooms
3 cups heavy cream
Salt & ground black pepper, to taste
Fried shoestring potatoes

1   Heat 1 tablespoon of the oil in a large skillet over medium heat. In batches, add the steak strips and cook, turning with tongs to brown evenly, until golden, about 1 minute per batch. (It's important to brown the steak in batches and give them room in the hot pan, otherwise they will release liquid and steam instead of brown.) Transfer the strips to a bowl as they brown and add additional oil as needed between batches.

2   Drizzle another 1 tablespoon olive oil into the pan and reduce the heat to low. Add the onions and sauté until wilted, about 3 minutes. Add the garlic and stir for just 1 minute, until fragrant. Stir in the tomato paste and ketchup and mix well.

3   Return the browned meat to the pan and add the Worcestershire sauce. Then gently mix in the mushrooms. Drizzle in the cream and season with salt and black pepper. Mix well and cook over medium heat until the liquid comes to a simmer. Cook for another 15 minutes, stirring occasionally, until the sauce thickens.

4   Serve the dish immediately with a side of white rice and top with fried shoestring potatoes.

Ruth's Hearty Lentil Soup

This hearty, flavorful dish not only brings good luck and prosperity for the new year, but the taste always reminds us of Grandma Ruth's house in Santa Barbara. Our more modern take is eating this soup with tortilla chips, or we serve it with thick slices of toasted sourdough bread with butter. Extra butter for Grandma!

SERVES 16

8 **cups** chicken stock
1 **(16-ounce) package** red lentils
2 ham hocks
1½ **cups** chopped celery
1½ **cups** chopped onions
1 to 1½ **cups** sliced carrots
1 **teaspoon** garlic powder

1 **teaspoon** dried thyme
1 **teaspoon** dried basil
1 **teaspoon** salt
1 **(14-ounce) package** kielbasa or turkey kielbasa, thinly sliced (or sliced ham, or cooked turkey or chicken, or shredded beef) and browned

1   In a large pot, combine the stock, lentils, and ham hocks and bring to a simmer over medium-high heat. Cook for 20 minutes, or until the lentils soften.

2   Add the celery, onions, carrots, garlic powder, thyme, basil, and salt and simmer for 20 minutes.

3   Add the kielbasa and simmer for 90 minutes, until thickened. (If soup is too thick, add water.)

4   Remove the ham hocks and discard. Ladle the soup into bowls and serve.

CHAPTER 7

After Party

If we are going to enjoy a dessert, we believe it should be "worth it"! From **Dot's Strawberry Cream and Custard "Birthday" Pie (see page 191)**, which was served on our mom's birthday every year in her childhood, to Dad's favorite semi-homemade **Doug's German Chocolate Cake (see page 205)**, still served on his birthday every year, this chapter is our collection of easy dessert favorites that are on repeat and that invoke plenty of recipe requests whenever we make them!

If we ask anyone to bring dessert to a family gathering or holiday, it is always David and Miriam. With Miriam's Brazilian background, she is our resident dessert creator—Sunday dinner doesn't feel complete without **Miriam's Brazilian Pudim de Leite (see page 196)**!—and David is always a willing taste tester and occasional baker, although we won't be sharing his most infamous cake in this cookbook. When he was eight years old, he apparently did something naughty and got in trouble because while our parents were taking their leisurely Sunday afternoon nap, he baked a cake, frosted it, and then woke them up to give them his lopsided cake, with the words "I'm Sorry" scrolled across. Although none of us remember why he was in trouble or how that cake tasted, it is definitely a Moore quality to communicate through food!

When it comes to entertaining, we often recommend outsourcing the baked goods and desserts to guests or a local bakery, but we continue to make these family-favorite dessert recipes, like our **No-Fail Peach Crisp (see page 203)** and our world-famous **Special Occasion Peanut Butter Bonbons (see page 189)** because they cannot be beat! Whether you are looking for a sweet treat to share with neighbors, a new favorite to bring to your Sunday dinners, or a perfect, crowd-pleasing dessert for your next backyard barbeque—for this we recommend Kristin's epic **Grilled Glazed Donuts (see page 207)**—these recipes are sure to be "worth it"!

Special Occasion Peanut Butter Bonbons

Growing up, on every holiday or special occasion, we would make these decadent no-bake peanut butter bonbons with our mom. Now we all love carrying on this tradition as our own children have taken over dipping the peanut butter balls into melted chocolate! These are a true labor of love, but worth it!

MAKES 60

2 **cups** creamy peanut butter
4 **cups** confectioners' sugar
1 **cup (2 sticks)** salted butter, softened
2 **teaspoons** vanilla extract

2 **(12-ounce) bags** milk or semisweet chocolate chips
2 **tablespoons** canola oil or coconut oil
1 **package** kebab sticks

1   In a medium bowl, use a hand mixer to mix the peanut butter, sugar, butter, and vanilla into a creamy dough. Cover and refrigerate for 1 to 2 hours, until the dough is firm.

2   Line two baking sheets with parchment paper. Take heaping tablespoons of dough and form into balls about 1 inch in diameter, rolling the dough in your hands to make all sides round. Place on the baking sheets. Repeat until you have used all of the dough. Freeze the balls for about 30 minutes, until hardened.

3   In a double boiler set over simmering water, melt the chocolate chips and the oil, stirring until combined. Reduce the heat to low so the water is only barely simmering. Using a kebab stick, dip each frozen dough ball into the chocolate to cover completely, then place back on the baking sheet. (If the chocolate starts to thicken in the bowl, turn the heat up for a minute or so, until the chocolate is warmed through.) Continue dipping each frozen dough ball until they all are covered in chocolate. Return the baking sheet to the fridge or freezer to set, about 30 minutes in the fridge or 15 minutes in the freezer. The bonbons, packed in an airtight container, keep well in the freezer or fridge for up to 14 days, but trust me they won't be there for long!

Dot's Strawberry Cream and Custard "Birthday" Pie

Our grandma Dot's famous strawberry pie was christened "Birthday Pie" because it was the dessert our mom requested every single year on her birthday, which was right during strawberry season. However, our parents were high school sweethearts, so our dad *also* loves this pie as it was what Grandma Dot served when he came over to visit our mom! A flaky pie crust is filled with a creamy, sweet custard that sets until it is silky smooth, then topped with fresh strawberry slices and a generous serving of whipped cream. It is the perfect summer treat!

SERVES 8–12

1 large egg yolk

2 large eggs

3 cups whole milk

1¼ **cups** granulated sugar

⅓ **cup** cornstarch

¼ **teaspoon** salt

3 tablespoons unsalted butter, cut into 3 pieces

1 tablespoon vanilla extract

1 baked pie shell (or baked store-bought pie crust; it's hard to beat Trader Joe's or Marie Callender's pie crust)

Fresh strawberries, sliced and sugared, for serving

Homemade whipped cream (a dash of cinnamon makes it special), for serving

1   In a small bowl, whisk together the egg yolk and eggs and set aside.

2   Whisk together the milk, sugar, cornstarch, and salt in a heavy pan. Place over medium heat and cook, stirring to prevent burning, for 5 minutes. Continue to cook, stirring, until the mixture comes to a gentle boil and thickens, 5 to 7 minutes. Do not rush the process; it will take up to 10 or 12 minutes total. Remove from the heat.

3   To temper the eggs, use a small measuring cup and remove about ¼ cup of the cooked milk mixture. While mixing briskly with a fork or whisk, pour a stream of the milk mixture into the bowl of beaten eggs. Repeat several times so that ¾ to 1 cup of the cooked milk is blended into the eggs. Return the tempered eggs to the hot milk in the saucepan and continue whisking until the milk mixture and eggs are thoroughly incorporated.

4 Place the saucepan back on the stove and cook the custard over medium heat until it comes to a boil again. Cook for about 2 minutes while continuing to stir/whisk, until thickened. Remove from heat and stir the butter and vanilla into the custard until the butter is melted and incorporated.

5 Pour the custard mixture into the pie crust. Put plastic wrap on top and press gently to prevent a film forming on the top of the custard. Refrigerate for several hours to completely cool. Serve with fresh whipped cream and strawberries!

Hot Fudge and Mint Chip Ice Cream Pie

After coming in sweaty from the sport court on hot summer afternoons, David and his friends would find this pie in the freezer and chip away at it—spoonful by spoonful—until it was all gone! A classic standby in the Moore family, we've tried several variations over the years, but always return to this one! You can whip it up for a summer barbecue, kid's birthday party, or Sunday dinner and it is always a hit with adults and kids alike.

SERVES 12

1 gallon green mint chip ice cream
1 (6-ounce) pre-made Oreo or chocolate cookie pie crust
1 (16-ounce) jar Mrs. Richardson's hot fudge, at room temperature

1   Slightly soften the ice cream at room temperature for about 10 minutes so that it is easy to smooth into the pie crust.

2   Gently layer the ice cream into the cookie crust and press down softly so that no air holes remain. Be careful not to break the crust. Flatten the top to accommodate the fudge topping, which you'll add later. Cover and place the pie in the freezer for several hours (or overnight) to thoroughly freeze.

3   Uncover the pie and top with almost the entire jar of room-temperature hot fudge. Return the pie to the freezer until thoroughly frozen again.

tip Switch the ice cream flavor to your favorite. Some of ours are coffee ice cream for a hula pie experience, chocolate chip cookie dough, and peppermint chip during the holidays. Try serving with fresh strawberries: The green, red, and chocolate brown palette is a sight for hungry eyes!

Miriam's Brazilian Pudim de Leite

Our family has benefited over and over again from Miriam and her delicious Brazilian recipes. Pudim is by far Brazil's favorite dessert, and like many Brazilian desserts, the secret to what makes it so good is sweetened condensed milk. Miriam has perfected the consistency and technique of her pudim, and it is now highly requested at every family function. For the best pudim, make a day ahead.

SERVES 12

1 cup granulated sugar
2 (14-ounce) cans Nestlé La Lechera sweetened condensed milk
14 ounces whole milk (use the condensed milk can to measure)
4 large eggs
2 tablespoons Nestlé Ninho dry milk (optional)

1 Preheat the oven to 360°F.

2 Spread the sugar in a 9-inch angel food cake pan and heat on the stove over medium heat until it turns into a caramelized syrup, about 3 minutes. Remove from the heat and turn and twist the pan so that the syrup covers the entire bottom and sides of the pan. Set aside until the syrup hardens.

3 In a blender, combine the condensed milk, whole milk, eggs, and dry milk and blend well on low speed for 1 minute. Carefully pour the milk mixture into the reserved caramel pan.

4 Create a water bath by pouring 1 inch of hot water into a large roasting pan. Place the angel food pan in the water bath and carefully transfer to the oven. Bake for 1 hour and 15 minutes, until wiggly like jello but set to the touch. Remove the cake from the water bath and let cool completely. Refrigerate for at least 2 hours, or up to 2 days, before serving. Just before serving, run the tip of a knife around the inside of the mold. Place a large plate over the mold and invert: the pudim should slide out. Spoon the remaining caramel sauce on top and serve.

The Perfect
Chocolate Chip Cookie

Chocolate chip cookies have truly brought our family even closer together. Doug once embarked upon a quest to find the perfect chocolate chip cookie, and David was his eager tester and relentless cheerleader. Together they tried and tested until Doug finally succeeded. For the last 17 years, this is the only chocolate chip cookie recipe Kristin will make!

MAKES 5 DOZEN

2 **cups (4 sticks)** salted butter, barely softened
1 **cup** granulated sugar
2 **cups** packed brown sugar
4 large eggs
2 **teaspoons** vanilla extract

6 **cups** all-purpose flour
1½ **teaspoons** salt
1½ **teaspoons** baking soda
1½ **(12-ounce) packages** really good milk chocolate chips

1   Preheat the oven to 375°F. Line several baking sheets with parchment paper.

2   In a medium bowl with a hand mixer, cream together the butter, sugars, eggs, and vanilla really well. Add the flour, salt, and baking soda and blend together only until combined (don't over mix). With a large spoon, stir the chocolate chips into the dough.

3   Roll the dough into 1-inch balls and place about 1-inch apart on the prepared baking sheets. Refrigerate for 20 minutes (this makes cookies that are thicker with a gooey inside).

4   Bake each sheet for 7 to 9 minutes in batches. The cookies will be golden brown on the outside but still pretty gooey on the inside when they are done.

Fabulous Cranberry Coconut Shortbread Cookies

We were introduced to this delicious cranberry coconut cookie recipe by our mom's friend Georgia. Although Georgia is no longer with us, we remember her fun, humorous, and sweet spirit whenever we make these delicious cookies! Packed with dried cranberries and coconut, these cookies are perfect staples for a holiday cookie plate or to package as party favors for a Christmas soirée!

MAKES 6 DOZEN

1½ **cups (3 sticks)** salted butter, softened

2 **cups** granulated sugar

2 **teaspoons** grated orange zest

2 **teaspoons** vanilla extract

3¼ **cups** all-purpose flour

1 **teaspoon** baking powder

¼ **teaspoon** salt

1½ **cups** dried cranberries

1½ **cups** sweetened coconut flakes

1 Preheat the oven to 350°F. Butter several 12x15-inch baking sheets.

2 In the bowl of a stand mixer, beat the butter, sugar, orange zest, and vanilla on medium speed until smooth. In a medium bowl, mix the flour, baking powder, and salt. Mix the dry ingredients into the butter mixture, then beat on a low speed until the dough comes together. Mix in the cranberries and coconut slowly until combined. Don't over mix.

3 Shape the dough into about 72 (1-inch) balls or use a cookie scoop to form the dough into balls. Place the balls about 2 inches apart on the prepared baking sheets, pressing each with a fork to flatten.

4 Bake on one cookie sheet at a time, in batches. Bake until the cookie edges just begin to brown, 8 to 11 minutes per batch (shorter baking time will yield a chewier cookie; longer baking time will yield a crispier cookie). Let the cookies cool on the baking sheets for 5 minutes. After the cookies are cool, use a wide spatula to transfer them to racks to cool completely. Store in an airtight container or freeze.

No-Fail Peach Crisp

Because Kristin hosts often but isn't a big baker, she is always looking for an easy, crowd-pleasing dessert. It doesn't get much easier than assembling sugared peaches in a massive cast-iron skillet, smothering them with a sweet and crunchy nutty oat topping, Traegering while everyone eats dinner, and then serving alongside vanilla ice cream! While we make this year-round, with all sorts of fruit, we especially love it during peach season!

SERVES 12

Topping
1½ cups old-fashioned oats
1 cup all-purpose flour
¾ cup packed brown sugar
½ cup granulated sugar
½ teaspoon cinnamon
½ teaspoon salt
¾ cup (1½ sticks) butter, cold
1 cup pecans, chopped, optional
2 tablespoons butter, softened

Filling
6 to 8 peaches, pitted and sliced, or
    2 (16-ounce) bags frozen peaches
¼ cup packed brown sugar
¼ cup granulated sugar
2 teaspoons lemon juice
1 teaspoon cinnamon

1 Set the Traeger to 350°F or preheat the oven. Smear the bottom of a 9x13-inch casserole dish or large cast-iron skillet with butter or cooking spray.

2 *For the topping:* Mix the oats, flour, brown sugar, granulated sugar, cinnamon, pecans (if using), and salt in a medium bowl. Rub in the butter with your fingers until clumps form and no dry spots remain.

3 *For the filling:* Toss the peaches, brown sugar, granulated sugar, lemon juice, cinnamon, and salt in a large bowl to combine. Transfer to the prepared dish and crumble the topping on top, breaking it into large pieces.

4 Bake the crisp until the topping is golden brown and the filling juices are thick and bubbling around the edges, 25 to 35 minutes.

Doug's German Chocolate Cake

As newlyweds in Rhode Island, Laurie baked Doug a triple-layer German Chocolate Cake and invited friends over to their third-floor walkup to celebrate! Ever since, Doug has requested German Chocolate Cake for his birthday!

SERVES 16

Cake

1 (15.25-ounce) package devil's food cake mix

1 (5.9-ounce) package instant chocolate pudding mix

1 cup vegetable oil

½ cup warm water

4 large eggs

1 cup sour cream

Frosting

1 cup evaporated whole milk (from a 12-ounce can)

1 cup sugar

3 large egg yolks

½ cup (1 stick) unsalted butter, softened

1 teaspoon vanilla extract

1⅓ cups sweetened coconut flakes

1 cup pecans, chopped

1 ***For the cake:*** Preheat the oven to 350°F. Grease the bottom of two 9-inch round cake pans.

2 Prepare the batter for the cake mix according to the directions with the vegetable oil, warm water, and eggs, and then add sour cream and pudding mix to the batter. Evenly divide the batter between the cake pans. Bake for a few minutes longer than the recommended baking time on the cake box directions to account for the sour cream. Let the layers cool for 10 to 15 minutes before removing from the pans.

3 ***For the frosting:*** Meanwhile, in a medium saucepan over medium heat, combine the milk, sugar, egg yolks, butter, and vanilla and stir until the frosting thickens, about 12 minutes. Remove the pan from the heat and stir in the coconut and pecans. Refrigerate the frosting until cold.

4 To frost the cake, place one of the cake layers on a serving stand or plate. Spread about half of the frosting on top of the layer. Add the second cake layer, and spread the top with the rest of the frosting. Thoroughly chill the cake for easier cutting.

Grilled Glazed Doughnuts

We weren't kidding when we said we love to Traeger just about everything! With Kristin and David being the only Moore siblings to live close by one another in Utah, they often spend time together grilling and usually end up discussing new foods to Traeger! One afternoon, Kristin asked David to bring over a box of store-bought glazed donuts to grill. The result was a donut which was crispy and sugary on the outside, soft and chewy on the inside, and reminiscent of elegant creme brûlée!

MAKES 12

1 dozen favorite glazed (yeast) doughnuts

Optional Whipped Cream and Strawberries
2 cups heavy cream
¼ cup confectioners' sugar
2 teaspoons vanilla extract
1½ teaspoons cinnamon
12 strawberries, thinly sliced, for garnish

1 Set the Traeger to 400°F and preheat with the lid closed for 15 minutes.

2 For the whipped cream: In a blender or a large bowl with a hand mixer, beat the cream, sugar, vanilla, and cinnamon until combined and whipped cream consistency. Set in the fridge until you are ready to use.

3 Place the doughnuts on the grill and cook for 2 to 3 minutes on each side, until glaze is bubbly and there are grill marks on the doughnuts. Serve right off the grill while the doughnuts are hot, topping with whipped cream and strawberries if you like. We love eating them plain as well!

tip One year, Kristin and Jeremy grilled donuts for Halloween instead of distributing candy. Before the night was over, the whole neighborhood was in the yard! ✎

Tips for Feeding a Crowd

When it comes to feeding a crowd, less is more. You're probably thinking, "But, there are *more* people, so don't I need *more*?!" Hear us out! The *less* you have to worry about, the better; the *less* food preparation you have to do on party day, the better **(see our How to Plan a Party section, page 225, for tips on preparing things in advance)**; and the *less* items you make from scratch, the better.

These tips will help turn party food preparation into something that is easy, delightful, and stress-free. This way you have more time to savor the special memories with family and friends—passing food around the table, clinking glasses, and hearing laughter throughout the house.

The joy is in the journey.
Turn on music. Get comfortable. Pour yourself a drink (Diet Coke for some of us). If prepping and planning for a crowd stresses you out and you're grumpy and quick-tempered with your family, pause. Reset. Think to yourself, "How can I make this more fun?" Then, do that! If you're on-edge and stressed, your crowd will feel that too. Relax, enjoy the process, and don't worry about details.

Celebrate both the homemade and the store bought!
If you make the best apple pie on the block or your grandmother's sweet potato casserole is to-die-for, put all your time and effort into those specific dishes. In all reality, convenience foods will lessen your stress. This is not the time to make your first pie crust or homemade dinner rolls. Stick with what you're good at and buy that amazing dessert from your local cake shop or those fresh dinner rolls from a favorite bakery.

Upgrade your favorite staple dish.
Jazz up boxed stuffing with fresh herbs and sausage. Add buttermilk fried onions to an otherwise bland green bean casserole. Add a small touch of homemade to your favorite store-bought item and your guests will never know it's not from scratch. **(For additional tips see our Shortcuts and Glam-Ups on page 218.)**

Focus on timing.

Prepare all your side dishes the day before! You'd be surprised how much can be done ahead of time. If you don't believe us, just try it! Sweet potato casserole can rest in the fridge for a day and be baked the day of; marinate your meat for your 4th of July barbecue ahead of time so it's ready for grilling; cut up your salad toppings and make the salad dressing ahead of time: those can easily store for a few days prior to your event. You'll be so happy the morning of your gathering when you wake up knowing 90% of your meal is done.

Start the night off with a tasty appetizer or specialty drink.

Apple cider, cream soda, and a little mint is a refreshing and festive way to welcome guests into your home. Little bites like bacon-wrapped dates or goat cheese stuffed mini pears are an easy and yummy way to begin the night. Tasty appetizers such as these aren't just for your guests! They benefit the cook too by letting people mingle and munch while you finish up in the kitchen.

Make it a potluck.

Don't underestimate the power of a potluck! Let your guests pitch in and show off their favorite dishes. Many hands make light work, and you all win when everyone brings something to the table.

Add filler foods.

Don't neglect filler foods—especially if you're feeding a lot of kids. Filler foods are a way to feed your guests more inexpensively and to ensure your guests and kids don't leave hungry. Some filler foods we regularly use are things like Costco Mac 'n cheese, a big bowl of spaghetti, or cheese pizza for kids at the buffet. You can also put out large bowls of grapes, crackers and cheese, your favorite rolls with butter and jam, or a big tray of carrots, celery, cucumber and ranch.

Get creative with leftovers.

You can use your leftover Sunday brisket and potatoes and add in peppers and eggs to make a breakfast hash the next morning. Throw leftover fruit into the freezer for smoothies. Use your Thanksgiving turkey, stuffing, and mashed potatoes in unique and fun ways: turkey soup with stuffing meatballs, Thanksgiving eggs Benedict, or mashed potato croquettes. Your family will look forward to the leftovers just as much as the big day!

FAVORITE ITEMS TO SCALE UP

SALADS

Salads are so easy to scale up because all you have to do is add more greens to bulk things up for a larger crowd. **Macho Salad (see page 80)** and **Apple Pecan Salad (see page 87)** are great salads for crowds. (Pro tip: If serving a salad for a crowd, stick to greens that don't wilt easily, like spinach and arugula.) Store an extra bag or a few heads of lettuce in your fridge. If your salad is running low at a party just add more lettuce to add more volume and to feed more people.

SHEET-PAN SIDES

We love a good sheet-pan side for a party. Whether it's **Crispy Smashed Potatoes (see page 146)** or **Coconut Curry Cauliflower (see page 143)**, sheet-pan sides are a great way to add some color to your spread and an easy way to cater to any kind of dietary needs.

CASSEROLES (ONE-DISH MEALS)

Grab a few of those large roasting pans and make **Laurie's Triple Layer Lasagna** recipe in bulk **(see page 172)** if you are hosting a dinner or our **Cinnamon French Toast Bake (see page 34)** if you are gathering for breakfast. These are great make-ahead options and then all you have to do is set the oven and let it bake on party day. Easy and delicious!

PROTEIN

Meat may seem like an overwhelming thing to scale up, but it's actually really easy! Just throw some extra chicken or ribs in your marinade and you are set. **Doug's Famous Baby Back Ribs (see page 118)** is our favorite go-to recipe for a large group. They are easy to scale up to serve more people *and* they make for an iconic focal point to your celebration (just remember to put out a pack of wipes for the mess)! You also can't go wrong with our **Million Dollar Bacon (see page 121)**. Who doesn't love bacon?!

Kristin's Snack Board Tips and Tricks

I f we had to host a last-minute gathering, we could whip up a snack board from any of our pantries in 10 minutes and be ready to go. Don't believe us? It's so easy!

Snack boards are the ultimate party hack—they are easy to make, perfect for large gatherings, and convenient to customize. Where charcuterie boards are typically associated with meats and cheeses, snack boards are a free-for-all! You name it, you can put it on a snack board!

Before you begin, let's go over a few tips to make your snack boards delicious and iconic.

Prioritize color.
While shopping for your snacks, try and buy the most colorful foods you can find and get an array of colors.

Use a variety of sizes.
Look for a mixture of big, small, and uniquely sized items to add excitement to your table. Leave some food whole or halved for show/color and cut up remaining pieces to eat. For instance, get pretzel rods or sticks instead of normal shaped pretzels. Add a whole pear or half of an apple for color and cut up the other half to eat.

Add something unusual.
Find a couple of unexpected or unusual snacks for a pop of color or interest. For example, add a sliced bright pink watermelon radish. You can add items that may or may not be eaten, such as whole artichokes, colorful heirloom tomatoes, fresh herbs, or tropical fruits. Peruse your produce aisle and find some fun things to surprise and delight.

Include a mix of healthy and indulgent items.
You want to appeal to all of your guests, so make sure everyone sees something they could nibble on. Add a mix of contrasting flavors, like salty and sweet, light and rich.

Use bowls.

Adding dips, sauces, and toppings in bowls can add another dimension to your snack board. These bowls can also help fill bare spots. A bowl of flavored salt, freshly cut herbs, and quartered lemons or limes can add a sophisticated flare. Try and use the same color of bowls when possible but feel free to mix up sizes.

Choose a theme and run with it.

You don't have to stick to cheese and meat for a fun snack board. Hot dog boards, toast boards, pasta boards, fruit and yogurt boards, sandwich boards, baked potato boards—there are so many great and unique options to try!

Don't skimp.

More is more so buy as many items as you can for a full board!

Use fillers as needed.

To reduce money spent, pick items that fill space. Don't underestimate the power of lemons or grapefruits cut in half and placed throughout your board. They add a pop of color and are great space fillers. Other options like crackers, chips, cookies, or snacks, like popcorn, are great, inexpensive fillers.

Focus on presentation.

You want this snack board to be the WOW factor of your party so take time to place everything neatly and mix up color, texture, and types of foods. If you have time, adding fresh herbs or edible flowers can take your board to the next level.

NOW THAT WE'VE COVERED SOME FAVORITE TIPS, LET'S CREATE A SNACK BOARD TOGETHER!

1 *Prepare your board or paper.* Roll out a long piece of craft paper or place multiple cutting boards down the middle of your table. You don't have to have any special boards for this if you don't have them —use what you have!

2 *Start in the center.* Start by laying out food items in the center of the board, filling in items on opposite sides (kitty corner) to each other, and working outwards.

3 *Create clumps.* Keep your items clumped together for a fuller feel. Try not to let your paper or board show through.

4 *Prioritize fancier foods.* Try laying out nicer or more expensive items first, then grabbing your cheaper fillers as needed.

5 *Make it yours.* As you are laying the food down, pretend you are an artist creating a masterpiece! Don't try and copy one you've seen. Make it your own and work with what you have. This is a great way to have fun as you prepare!

6 *Enjoy!* Welcome your guests and watch their eyes light up!

CHEESES
Swiss cheese, cheddar cheese, American cheese, goat cheese, fresh mozzarella cheese.

DELI MEATS
pepperoni slices, ham, turkey, roast beef, prosciutto. (Roll up deli meats for visual effect.)

CRACKERS/CHIPS
piles of Ritz crackers, Triscuits, Wheat Thins, pretzels (any variety), bagel chips, potato chips.

UNIQUE ITEMS FOR VISUAL VARIETY
different types of olives for color, whole banana peppers, whole artichokes.

FILLERS
bowls of chip dips, cherry tomatoes, or olives.

FUN FRUITY BOARD

FRUIT OPTIONS
lemon halves (great way to fill space), raspberries, cherries, blackberries, blueberries, strawberries, grapes, and so on.

FILLERS
bowls of Nutella, caramel dipping sauce, a yogurt/cream cheese fruit dip

UNIQUE ITEMS
white chocolate chips or roughly chopped chocolate bark; dragon fruit, star fruit or passion fruit; sprigs of fresh mint leaves

SUGAR SWEET BOARD

CHOCOLATES
Choose a few chocolate options like mini Reese's cups, Rolos, Milk Duds, Junior Mints.

GUMMIES
Balance the chocolate with some gummy candies like Sour Patch Kids, peach rings, gummy worms or gummy bears, sour candy ropes.

FILLERS
With candy boards, the easiest fillers are bowls with small candies like M&Ms, Reese's Pieces, or Skittles.

FUN, UNIQUE ITEMS
Try fun, random candies like ring pops, lollipops, or gummy burgers.

BOUNTIFUL BREAKFAST BOARD

CARBS
Try a bagel board with different types of large or mini bagels; or a French toast board with French toast strips; or mini sweet rolls or muffins.

FRUIT
Whenever you can, add a pop of color with fruit: strawberries, rasp-berries, and blueberries are great options for a breakfast board.

FILLERS
bowls of cream cheese flavors, a bowl of cinnamon sugar, a bowl of syrup, etc.

PROTEIN
sausage links or bacon; hard-boiled eggs, cut in half

Shortcuts and Glam-Ups

K ristin, Tiffany, and Danielle have gotten good at adjusting their party prep while being busy moms. Let's face it— it's hard to make *all* the food at home! Don't let that stop you from gathering and bringing people together around your table. The Moores have years of practice, plenty of Food Network viewing under their belts, and some happy discoveries in all their years of hosting to help create a tricks and cheats list to make any store-bought item feel homemade. Start by making a few homemade favorites and then rely on store-bought items to finish things off.

QUESTIONS TO ASK YOURSELF

What do I make? What should I delegate or buy?

When deciding what to spend the most time on, focus on your strengths! If you are a baker at heart, make the time-intensive birthday cake or the decadent pie and assign out the appetizer to your guests. If you are a master griller, make the grilled chicken or steak and assign friends an accompanying recipe or let them bring their own favorite side dish. If there is a portion of the meal you care most about, focus on that and delegate or buy your way out of the rest.

What's the best way to delegate food items?

When inviting, do your best to relay to your guests what you will be making and how they can help! This is as easy as saying, "We'll be grilling the meat! Could you bring your favorite salad to share?" You can also let your guests know that grabbing some store-bought dip and chips or a veggie tray on the way over is just as good as our **Fired-Up Jalapeno Poppers (see page 65)**, because it actually is.

How do I incorporate store-bought items?

Anything that can help cut down on prep time is helpful! See more of our favorite shortcuts in the lists below.

Don't make hosting a time to show off, one-up, or run yourself ragged trying to make it all perfect—none of your guests expect perfection. Be a present-over-perfect and burnt-bread-over-stressed-out hostess by letting go and having fun! Your guests will feel it and follow suit. As much as people love seeing an elaborate homemade element, they love seeing how you turned that store-bought soup into something restaurant-worthy even more! This makes people think "Oh, I can do this too!"

What can we say? Fake it 'til you make it—or don't make it! (We won't tell if you won't!) Here are some of our favorite shortcuts and glam-ups:

ADD & EMBELLISH

Go nuts!
Toast any type of nuts in a sauté pan. Then simply chop and sprinkle on your store-bought salads or dips for extra fresh flavor and crunch. (Bonus tip: Put extra in the freezer to whip out in a hurry!)

Make the soup your own.
Top store-bought soups with croutons or breadcrumbs, add a drizzle of fresh cream or olive oil, or sprinkle with freshly shaved cheese or chopped herbs. (Bonus tip: This also works with store-bought lasagna or pasta.)

Freshen up with fresh herbs.
We can't say enough about chopped fresh herbs! They liven up any dish. Top store-bought dips, salads, breads—really anything—with fresh herbs to kick everything up a notch. Our favorites are cilantro, flat-leaf parsley, fresh chives, green onions, and rosemary.

Sprinkle with seasonings.
Top your store-bought hummus, dips, or guacamole with some finishing salt, flavorful seasoning combinations, or a drizzle of flavored olive oil or balsamic vinegar/glaze. We love Sriracha seasoning, seasoned salt, and everything but the bagel seasoning.

Keep berries on hand.
Adding a handful or two of different colored berries on top of store-bought cakes, cheesecakes, or any dessert magically creates more interest and flavor. Lemon curd is another yummy addition to store-bought desserts.

Dust with sugar.
A little bit of powdered sugar or turbinado sugar is the perfect touch on store-bought cake. You can also add edible flowers or melted icing for extra flare.

Pile with Parmesan.
Make store-bought pizza look homemade with a generous pile of shredded Parmesan cheese, fresh arugula, or chili flakes. Finish it off with a drizzle of olive oil and balsamic glaze and no one is the wiser!

Liven up your rice.
We love Trader Joes frozen brown rice. The best way to give it (or Minute Rice) new life is by adding fresh herbs, citrus (a squirt of fresh lemon or lime does wonders!), or even chunks of feta or pomegranate seeds. Rice doesn't need to be bland!

Jazz it up.
Jazz up a jar of alfredo sauce by adding Dijon mustard, hot sauce, bacon pieces, salt and pepper, chives, or a splash of lemon juice.

Give a glossy finish.
Brush store-bought pies (sweet or savory) with beaten egg and finish off in the oven (according to recipe directions) for a glossy look.

It's all about the drizzle.
Drizzle a bit of olive oil, chili oil, or balsamic vinegar on your platter or serving plate before adding your store-bought items. This makes a beautiful statement and creates the homemade effect.

CUT DOWN ON TIME

Shorten chopping time with scissors.
Get a great pair of sharp kitchen shears to cut lettuce, fresh herbs, meat, and more! Scissors can be such a quick, easy way to "chop" ingredients.

Trader Joe's to the rescue.
Trader Joe's can help cut cooking time in half with some products. We love frozen garlic cubes, bags of pre-chopped white onion, and pre-chopped mirepoix for soups, hashes, and sheet-pan veggies. (If you don't have a Trader Joe's nearby, you can find similar items at regular grocery stores.)

If able, buy pre-washed, pre-cut, or bagged items.
If time and energy are in short supply, buy as many of your vegetables pre-chopped, pre-cut, and pre-bagged at the grocery store. It's much easier to make things when you literally dump them in the frying pan or on the cookie sheet and cook right away rather than spending time washing, drying, and slicing.

Pull out the slow cooker.
If you don't have time to cook, throw a handful of ingredients in a crockpot or pressure cooker and have a meal ready for your family. This works for chicken fajitas, pulled pork, shredded beef, and more!

Fire up the grill or Traeger!
Heat up store-bought items on your Traeger or grill to add flavor. Store-bought pizzas, meats, casseroles, really anything that goes in your oven is *so* much better on

a Traeger (which is essentially an outdoor oven). We are big fans of Papa Murphy's pizzas and store-bought cookie dough on the Traeger **(see our I'd Smoke That! Our Favorite Traeger'd Additions on page 139)**.

Double the protein, double the yum.
Always make twice as much protein as you need and then use it in different ways later in the week. For example, we love cooking a whole chuck roast on the Traeger and dividing it into multiple bags to freeze and use on salads, in wraps, or on top of nachos.

OUTSOURCE FOR IDEAS

Google it.
Have a ripe avocado, tomato, and chicken in your fridge? Search "recipes with avocado, chicken, and tomato." This can work with a dish you loved at a restaurant as well.

Use your local grocery store salad bar for specific ingredients.
If there's an element you need for a dish that you don't want to cook up (crumbled cooked bacon or marinated ahi tuna, for example), buy it from the salad bar instead

of frying it up. We do this often for ahi tuna, bacon, chicken, beets, hard-boiled eggs, and croutons.

Get inspiration from food bars.
Peruse your local grocery store salad bars or food bars for ideas of what to cook at home to help mix things up. This is a perfect visual and smell test for what might look good to you and your family. But make it at home! It is much cheaper than buying pre-prepped food by the pound when buying for a family.

Hopefully these shortcuts and glam-ups will help you realize that you don't *have* to do everything yourself! And don't be afraid to share your shortcuts! We are the first to brag to our guests that, yes, we did, in fact, buy all these dips from the store (after they had already taken a bite and raved about the flavors, all jumping to get the recipes).

NAIL THE PRESENTATION

Stack it up, fan it out, slice it up.
We eat with our eyes first and good presentation makes even store-bought food yummier.

Pile high.
Make a regular recipe a masterpiece by serving elements piled together rather than spread out separately. Doing a rice bowl? Layer the rice, then sweet potatoes, then black beans and top with chicken and additional toppings. Always start with carb, then veggie, with protein on top.

Keep things odd.
Serving an odd number of elements on your plate is more visually appealing.

Never serve in store-bought containers.
Always take food out of their containers and serve on a platter, in a bowl, or in your own baking dish.

Make it a bowl.
Bowls have no rules. Start with any sort of rice or carb on the bottom, add a protein, veggies of any sort, fruit of any sort, nuts of any sort. Then drizzle with a sauce and you have dinner!

It's all about the mixed greens.
Use 2 to 3 types of bagged lettuce for your salad for a mix of texture, color, and flavor.

How to Plan a Party

Whether you are new to party planning or are a seasoned event planner, we are sharing an ultimate party-planning timeline to help you minimize the stress and maximize the fun with your next gathering!

This timeline is so helpful when you are preparing for a large, formal party (think family reunion, barbecue, baby shower, bridal shower, graduation party, retirement party, etc.). If you are throwing a spontaneous gathering in the next day or two (or hour or two!), then ditch this list, pull out your platters and get cracking!

TWO MONTHS OUT

1 *Pick a theme.*
Is this a holiday party? Find a fun theme (or color) to be the focal point. This could be as easy as doing a Winter Wonderland Christmas party or a Pretty in Pink Galentine's Day party.

You can use a picture, item, or color scheme as your inspiration—such as your team's colors for a Super Bowl party or a fun picture you saw on Pinterest for your upcoming girls' luncheon. It's your party, so pick something you get excited about!

2 *Pick a date.*
When it comes to selecting a date, consider a day of the week that will work best for your guests. Look at your school's event calendar, your community's event calendar, and especially consider any local sporting programs in your area (unless you are centering your party around one of those events). Talk to your friends or family to make sure there aren't any scheduling conflicts you are missing.

The biggest party-planning mistake is to schedule your party on a very busy night for your friends or family. In all our hosting experience, we find that Thursday nights work best for girlfriend gatherings, Saturday nights are great if you are inviting couples, and Sunday nights are great for family "Sunday Suppers" where everyone is invited.

3 *Create your guest list.*
Whether you are hosting a small dinner party, a larger girls' night, or a family barbecue, getting a tentative guest list together ahead of time is a great idea. Talk to your spouse, partner, or co-host and coordinate the guest list together.

• Don't try to invite *everyone*! As nice as it would be, you simply cannot invite everyone. It's okay to invite some people one time and other people another time. Just try and make sure each family or guest knows at least 1 to 2 other families or guests in attendance. Not everyone has to know everyone!

• It's not about a circle of friends, but a horseshoe. So many of us have circles of friends (family, extended family, high school friends, college roommates, etc.) that are closed. When we close ourselves off to meeting new people, we limit ourselves. Instead, open up your circle; open up your life, your family, your home and invite more people in. It's amazing how much richer our lives become when we invite people into them who look differently than us, think differently than us, and have different backgrounds, lifestyles, or religions. This diversity enhances our lives.

4 *Start gathering supplies and/or decorations.*
Find pictures around the color and/or theme of your party for inspiration. The more time you have to think about and research party ideas, the easier it will be to spark your creativity and get those party-planning juices flowing.

Start gathering party favors, decorations, plastic plates/cutlery/napkins ahead of time so you aren't scrambling for those elements at the last minute.

ONE MONTH OUT

1 *Plan your menu*.
Yes, you can totally plan your menu this far in advance! Here are some things to considering when picking your menu:

• *Season*. This is a great way to narrow down options for what you can serve. If it's a fall party, then cozy foods like **Laurie's Triple Layer Lasagna (see page 172)** or **Christine's Classic Minestrone Soup (see page 171)** are great options. If it's a summer barbecue, then our **Traeger'd Favorites chapter** will be your best friend **(see page 109)**. Start by picking cozy, warm foods for the cooler months and light, refreshing foods for the warmer months.

• *Setting*. Are your guests going to be sitting at the table or relaxing on picnic blankets outside? This can affect whether food can be messy or needs to be handheld.

• *Guests.* Is this a ladies' luncheon? Then lighter food options are probably best. Preparing a grill-out for your husband's friends? Then double the meat and double the sauce, my friend. Hosting a kid's birthday party or teen's friend group? Then you'll want to cater to those younger audiences, asking your kids what they are hoping for and wanting to plan for the party. Have your kids get involved in the menu selection (we often end up with Panda Express) and the kids are happy!

• *Presentation.* When deciding your menu, we don't want all the food to be the same color or texture. Items that have a pop of color are a great way to create visual interest.

TWO WEEKS OUT

1 *Send out invitations and ask for an RSVP.*
For a more formal party, you can opt for printed invites. Who doesn't love getting an invite in the mail or hand-delivered to their door? But if that isn't for you (or you don't want the extra work), then embrace the evite! Sending electronic invitations via email, paperless post, or text is quick and easy for you and makes it easy for people to email or text their RSVP.

2 *Assess what items you DO have.*
If you're using your own dishes, make sure you have enough of everything.

• For hosting big gatherings, we highly recommend using sturdy paper or plastic plates, plastic glasses, and either regular silverware or plastic cutlery. When party time comes, you will be so glad you can dump everything in the trash and not have to spend time slaving away at the sink, washing a million dishes. Trust us.

• If you need more of anything, now is the time to head to the store and grab another set of plastic cups, stock up on napkins, or get another box of plastic cutlery.

Make sure you know what your serving table will look like and what you will need for it. Will you be serving cans of sodas in a large cooler with ice or do you need

a drink dispenser for your serving table? Do you have platters for serving your salads or sides?

• Walk around your house and start gathering any tablecloths, vases, decorative place mats, etc. that you'll want to use to liven up your serving area.

• If you don't have everything you need, now is a great time to stop by the store, order something online, or check with your neighbors or friends to see if you can borrow anything.

By doing this two weeks ahead of time, you are gradually eliminating the chance of party-induced stress at a later date.

3 *Plan activities to create interest (optional).*
Sometimes it can be fun to give your guests something to do at your party. This can be as easy as setting up different stations for your menu items: a drink station, food station, and dessert station. This keeps your guests moving and engaged while they mingle from area to area. Don't overthink this. It can be as

simple as three different tables (if you have them) or simply placing drinks on the snack bar, food on the dining table and dessert on the coffee table.

• Turning your stations into a "make your own" is another great way to give people something to do while they mingle. Some ideas can be to make your own mocktail, yogurt parfait, baked potato or taco bar, or a s'mores station. Get creative! This is also a great way for you to have less assembling or preparation since your guests will do it themselves!

• Another favorite activity option is to lay out cards and pens for people to write notes on—or cards with printed questions for conversation starters.

• Turning your parties into an opportunity to serve others is an amazing way to bring people together for a bigger purpose. If your friends are coming over for a girls' luncheon, set up some stations for tying blankets for your local children's hospital. Planning a kid's birthday party? Invite guests to bring gifts to donate to a state children's program. There are so many great ways to serve within your community—and having your guests help will be fulfilling for them, too!

• If you are looking for some type of entertainment for your guests, have a friend who's great at painting nails come and do a quick coat on each of your friends' nails. You could set up a photo booth with props and have a friend who's a great photographer come and take pictures. Do you have an artsy friend? Invite them to come and do face-painting or sketches-to-order for your guests. Does one of your kids play an instrument? "Hire" them to play some live music for your guests (FYI, this is a great incentive to get your kids to practice their instrument, too!).

You don't have to spend a lot of money to have unique, fun "activities" at your party. Choose something that works for the type of gathering you are hosting and the people who are coming. And think outside the box! Whatever you choose, your guests will have so much fun! But give yourself time to prepare and schedule things by planning it out at least two weeks in advance.

4 *Pick out what you're going to wear (seriously)!*
These are the little things you're not going to want to worry about as the date gets closer! If you know what you're going to wear ahead of time, then you'll make sure it's steamed and ready to go.

5 *Hire help.*

Arrange babysitting for 2 hours before the party and during the party. Also consider hiring a "helper" for the party itself. You pay for babysitters, so why not pay for help during the party and for a couple of hours before and after. It will be worth every cent, and you'll feel less stressed during the event.

THREE DAYS OUT

Hit the grocery store.

Buy drinks, non-perishables, and most of the food (except bread or things that may go stale).

TWO DAYS OUT

Start your food prep!

Prepare most of your food and store it in baggies so it's ready to go. Ziplock bags are your best friends when preparing food for large gatherings. You can really do most things two days before:

- Cut up the toppings for your salad
- Make your salad dressing or marinade
- Prepare any dips or sauces
- Marinate your meat
- Toast the nuts for the salad
- Brown and chop bacon for bacon bits

Hold off on preparing the following until the day of:

- Tomatoes
- Avocados
- Tossing your salad with the salad dressing

1 *Buy remaining grocery items.*
Whatever items you wanted to hold off on, now is the time to go get them! You don't want to be running to the store the morning of the party. (P.S., if that *does* happen, send someone else!)

2 *Set up the serving area.*
Set out all platters with slips of paper on each saying where food goes. Lay out your plates, napkins, silverware, and cups where they should be.

3 *Chill your drinks.*
If you are serving cans of soda, liters of lemonade, etc., put them in the fridge. If you are making a homemade drink, you can make it a day ahead (even homemade drinks that include soda mixed in — you can usually make an element of the recipe ahead of time and then add the carbonation just before serving).

4 *Set up decorations.*
If using fresh flowers, you can buy flowers the day before and arrange them. Keep them in a cool room or in the fridge for best results.

1 *Get dressed and ready.*
We always get dressed and ready to go 2 to 3 hours before the party. You'll feel much better if you are ready to go and can still mingle with your guests as they arrive while you finish off this or that—you can't mingle with your guests as they arrive if you are stuck in the bathroom frantically getting ready because you prioritized the remaining prep.

2 *Finish food preparation.*
Since you made sure everything that could be done ahead of time was done

ahead of time, preparing the remaining food the morning of the party should be much easier to manage.

• We like to have platters, a buffet line-up of silverware, dishes, napkins, drink dispensers, and florals or tablescapes set out hours before the party.

• Food can be set out 20 to 30 minutes before. I like to have most food items at room temperature and just one or two that need to be hot (or cold).

• Drinks can be set out and left at room temperature if you have an ice canister available during the party. You can also place ice in a cooler and let your drinks rest in there ahead of time so they are cold for the event.

• Salads can easily be enjoyed at room temperature—so don't stress about keeping those cold.

• Rolls don't have to be served hot or warm, so set those out in advance (just keep them covered or contained until party time so they don't dry out).

• Meats should be served hot or warm, so keep that in mind when cooking them and how you want to serve them. If you are grilling during the event, then this won't be a problem. If you want to prepare the meat ahead of time, then keep your oven on warm and pull out a hot tray of meat as needed.

• All desserts (except frozen desserts) can be enjoyed at room temperature. Lay out your dessert table ahead of time and then forget about it.

3 *Set out last minute details.*
Pull the flowers out of the fridge, turn the music on, light the candles, and set out any remaining finishing touches. Give yourself a good 15 to 20 minutes before the beginning of your event since there are always people who arrive early. If you still have finishing touches to add when guests start arriving, invite them to help you out! Everyone loves lending a hand. This way you can finalize things without feeling like you aren't giving your recently arrived guests a proper welcome.

All food does not have to be done, but make sure you have something for your guests to eat and drink and that you have your lipstick on at "go" time.

Thanks to all your preparation, you are calm, cool, and collected when your guests arrive, and you are ready (and able) to have a great time! If you're happy and "chill," that's how your party will be. Your guests will mirror your energy or emotion for the party. If you're running around like crazy and feeling stressed, everyone will feel it. That's why it's so important to take care of as many of the elements ahead of time so when the time comes, you can mingle with your guests, eat, drink, and take it easy because all the hard work is behind you and you're ready to party!

Showing Up
and Giving Back

*There is no other place we would rather give of our time and talents
than around the table.*

As delicious as this collection of recipes is, the true purpose in feeding is not in the physical food itself, but in the moments we experience as a result of sharing a meal. Sitting together at a table to laugh, learn, and listen is a tradition as ancient as humanity itself and one we embrace enthusiastically. Simply, eating together builds camaraderie and relationships. Whether we are family or friends, acquaintances or neighbors, or community members or colleagues, sharing a meal builds connections.

Throughout our childhood, we watched our parents show up in big and small ways. They taught us that "where much is given, much is required," and they emulate this mantra in how they live their lives. Although a yearning to serve is woven into the Moore DNA, we each do so in different ways. In fact, our approaches are so varied that Kristin was inspired to create a way for us to each identify our own Giving Personality! **(see chart on page 238)** Not only has this insight helped us better appreciate each other's interests and talents, it helps us better navigate our own journeys toward integrating service into our daily lives.

Inviting others to our table, whether we cook an elaborate spread or set takeout onto the counter, is our family's favorite way to serve. Food allows us to give of our time and talents. As we come to the table, let down our guard, and take the time to connect, our souls are nourished as well as our bodies. By providing nourishment, even if only for an hour or an afternoon, we can give our attention and presence to those who are not only most deserving, but also need it most.

At our table, voices are heard and valued. Ideas are shared. Advice is given. We come to the table not to argue, defend, or boast, but to listen and be listened to. At our

table, everyone from the downtrodden, lonely, struggling, and meek to the confident and energetic are treated as queens and kings. All are alike and all are loved. At our table, we hope you feel a reprieve from the burdens of life.

ESTABLISH A CULTURE OF SERVICE

Because serving and sharing is ingrained in us, we have each found our unique way to contribute, from our tiny spheres of influence to our wider communities, as we try and lift our little piece of the world every single day.

We know that service starts in our own homes. We also know that when we look beyond ourselves and serve outside of our "bubble," we experience the richness of life to its fullest. Though our calendars may be full with more formalized activities, such as mentoring kids and cooking at a community center, we know that the small acts of service—a conversation, kind note, or generous thought mentioned— share light, lift those around us, and infuse a deep sense of joy and purpose into our lives.

Gathering for Impact

GIVING PERSONALITIES

We all give back to our families, communities, and the world in different and unique ways. As you read these descriptions of various Giving Personalities, find the one that best describes the way you would like to make an impact.

MENTOR/TEACHER

A person with a "Mentor/Teacher" giving personality is driven by a deep-seated desire to share knowledge, offer guidance, and help others grow. They enjoy contributing to the growth and development of individuals and communities, fostering a culture of learning and support.

KINDNESS SPREADER

A person with a "Kindness Spreader" giving personality focuses on fostering positive and supportive relationships and creating a warm, inclusive environment through acts of kindness and community involvement. Their efforts are often centered around making a tangible difference in their immediate surroundings, building a sense of community, and promoting well-being through simple yet meaningful acts of kindness and support.

CRISIS RELIEVER

A person with a "Crisis Reliever" giving personality is characterized by their ability to step in during urgent or challenging situations to provide immediate and practical support. They excel at addressing pressing needs and quickly managing immediate needs.

CULTURAL ENTHUSIAST

A person with a "Cultural Enthusiast" personality is deeply committed to and passionate about the arts, culture, and diversity. They often engage in charitable activities that celebrate and help enrich the cultural fabric of their communities to foster greater appreciation and understanding of diverse artistic and cultural expressions.

INFRASTRUCTURE ENHANCER

A person with an "Infrastructure Enhancer" personality is focused on improving and supporting the foundational systems and tools that enable structural and sustainable change. Their charitable efforts typically center around creating, optimizing, and maintaining the systems that facilitate long-term impact.

CHANGE AGENT

A person with a "Change Agent" giving personality is driven by a commitment to identify problems and implement solutions that result in systemic and meaningful change. Their efforts often focus on identifying critical issues, addressing root causes, creating transformative impacts across communities, and fostering sustainable progress.

TRUTH SEEKER

A person with a "Truth Seeker" giving personality is deeply committed to exploring, understanding, and communicating their personal beliefs and truths. This often involves a quest for authenticity and a desire to challenge and reshape existing narratives. Their charitable efforts frequently focus on promoting transparency, advocating for justice, and fostering a deeper understanding of critical issues.

CONVENER/GATHERER

A person with a "Convener/Gatherer" giving personality is focused on bringing people together to achieve collective goals and make a positive impact in their communities. They excel at organizing, mobilizing, and fostering collaboration among diverse groups to drive social change and community improvement.

FLEXIBLE SERVANT

A person with a "Flexible Servant" giving personality excels in adapting to various roles to meet the evolving needs of others effectively. Their ability to step into different roles makes them versatile and impactful in a wide range of charitable activities. People who have changing life circumstances or personal seasons often enjoy being a Flexible Servant.

In our family, we seek out "sticky service," an issue or cause that we care deeply about. Sticky service is something that speaks to us on a deeper level and keeps us coming back time and again. Sticky service is not about a single "service project," but about weaving a culture of service into our family. It is about integrating experiences into our lives that make us better people, while also contributing our time, talents, and resources to build our families and communities.

Identifying your "sticky service," may take time and patience. Which is okay—this is a long-term investment in your family culture! These actions might help you:

Investigate

First, investigate. Research topics that are relevant to your family. Read about, subscribe to emails, and follow on social media different nonprofits and organizations that you think your family might like! Ask your kids for ideas of people or causes they care about. Be reflective and introspective about what matters to you and choose something that resonates with your own family's ethos. There is no shortage of needs!

Participate

Second, show up and participate. Then, spend time weekly or monthly discussing these organizations. Try to understand the problems they face and how you can help become part of the solution, not only by meeting critical needs, but by tackling needs upstream to eliminate the problem altogether. Evaluate, pivot, and keep showing up until you find your "sticky service"!

Return

Third, return. The benefit in choosing something that matters to you is that you can't help but go back. We like to say, "Don't spend your time trying to save the whales if you don't care about the whales!" When we choose something we don't care about, it's less likely to stick, and is therefore less likely to change our hearts. So, choose something that matters to you. Finding family-friendly, hands-on service opportunities that coincide with the causes you care about—places where you can get your "hands dirty and hearts broken"—is a great investment in your family.

Sign up. Show up. And then return again and again. This is when the magic happens!

Lastly, include these experiences in dinnertime conversations, prayers, and holidays—become their champion. Invite others to join you. Stay open-minded and curious. As your seasons of life change or your family changes, don't be afraid to find a new way to serve.

As Moores, we believe that service is "not what we do but who we are."

Life can be beautiful and hard, lovely and heartbreaking. Our family has experienced our fair share of tribulations and have grown closer and stronger because of them. In publishing this book, it was important that we found a way to give back. We knew we wanted to focus on a cause that has touched our lives deeply.

Like many other families, ours has been impacted by addiction and substance abuse, a disease which has affected our family across most branches for decades. We have decided to give the proceeds of this book to an organization which focuses on substance abuse education and prevention.

Our brother David has struggled with this disease his entire adult life. We know how fortunate we are that David, through his own resilience and determination, prayers and faith, is still with us, thriving and healthy. To us, his life represents a beacon of hope. Now, he shares his story to not only help others as they battle this disease too, but also to highlight the critical role of transparent substance abuse education and prevention.

David's message is simple: The opposite of addiction is not sobriety; the opposite of addiction is connection. Connection is prevention! Connection heals deep wounds and gives us the support and understanding we need to recover. This book is a joyful way to share how we have used food to connect, build, and maintain relationships with those around us.

We hope through inviting others to your table, you can do the same.

Index

MIRIAM AND DAVID

KRISTIN AND JEREMY

Meet the Moore Family

DOUG AND LAURIE

DANIELLE AND PARIN

TIFFANY AND MATTHEW

*This is the power of gathering: it inspires us—delightfully—to be more hopeful,
more joyful, more thoughtful: in a word, more alive.*

ALICE WATERS

Thank You!

8-10 min.

Snappy Lemon
1/4 Soy sauce
2T. Wine
T. lemon

Hawaiian
1/3 c Soy sauce
1T

Butter Bonbons
powdered sugar
soft butter
peanut butter
chopped walnuts (optional)
vanilla
pkg. milk choc. chips
wax thin strip 2 T. oil

German Choc. Cake + Frosting
white cake mix
inst. choc pudding
eggs
milk

German
cake mix + 1/2 sour cream

Fondue - Cheese
2 tbs. kirsch
flt.   2 gm 1 swiss
3 lb cheese - cheddar, sharp
1 litre wine - 2/3 oz wine in pot
have garlic, rub garlic
almost boil - not boil

Ruthiebelle's Baked Stuffed Clams
4 lbs. minced clams
1/2 " bacon   1 can (15 oz) italian season br. cru.
2 1/2 " onions   salt, pepper, accent,
Grind each above separately + cook (simmer)   garlic powder, Parmesan cheese
approx. 20 min. mix ground clams + juice, drained
+ drained onion, + br. crumbs. salt, pepper
garlic powder, + cheese to taste
with clam juice if needed (too dry)
clam shells. Bake at 350°   makes 2   my own recipe

Stuffed Mushrooms
seasoned bread crumbs
margerine
chopped olives
bacon bits (real)
lg. mushrooms
Pull off mushroom stems + chop fine. saute in
margerine. Add bacon, seasoned bread crumbs
olives, bacon, + some reserved bacon drippings
May need to add additional water - to moisten
mixture. Stuff in mushroom caps. Bake at
350 x 20 min 'til hot + browned.

Sue Fields

of foil on shallow roasting pan.
smoke over + under meat (3 1/2 oz bottle).
6 hrs @ 250°
liquid smoke
hours (optional)
baste with sauce every 15 min during last hour.

Simmer:
1 tsp oregano
1 tsp margoram   use extra sauce
tsp sweet basil   on baked potatoes
tsp pepper   slice meat thinly
                         after it sits
sauce   for 15 minutes
sugar
salad oil

1/4 c. brown sugar
1 can corned beef
1T. vinegar

to taste ≈ 1T.

hamburger
d. onion
water
c. catsup

Brown hamburger. Add rest of ingredients
Simmer 1 hr. Serve on hamburger buns.

Ck. breasts 2013
1½ lbs. ck. breasts
1 pk. brocoli frozen cooked (slightly)
1 can cr. of ck. soup   sm. pieces
½ c. mayo
sauce ½ t. lem. juice
½ t. curry powder
cheese on top 1-1½ c.
½ c bread crumbs } mixed
1 T butter

25 min. - 350°
barely grease casserole
place cooked froz. Broc.
ck. on top of Broc - par-boil - skin off
small pieces (eve)

Sift eggs S
Beat eggs S
grad cold sugar - fold in
on juice - turn
well greased - flanel nuts on top
15 min. - turn
sprinkle nuts on top
roll

Choc. Chip Cookies   350°

1 C shortening }
2 c sugar   } cream
1 c Br. "   }
2 t. vanilla   }

3 eggs
2 t. salt
2 t. soda
3 C flour   2½   1 c oat
6 - 12 oz choc. chips

Cream Pie (mother's)
¼ c. cornstarch
⅔ c. sugar
tsp. salt
2 c. milk scalded
3 slightly beaten yolks
2 tbs. butter
½ tsp. vanilla extract
1 9 in. baked pie shell
3 stg beat

Mix cornstarch, ⅔ c sugar & salt
and add milk. Cook in
dbl. boiler til thick, about 10
min, stirring constantly.
Slowly add hot mixture to
egg yolks, stir into m.
hot mixture

---

2 eggs
2 eggs
5-6 cups

...milk with shortening, sugar, s...
...es in lukewarm water. When milk...
...en eggs. Add flour to make a s...
...juice. Roll out and spread dough...
(white or brown) add raisins o...
cinnamon. Roll up like jelly ro...
...ch thick. Pi... greased pan...
...led in bu...   about 15-...

shortening
sugar
salt

While
frostin...

Bacon & Egg Bake   Serves 6
                great for brunch
8 bacon slices
2 med. onions, sliced
1 can. cr. of mush soup
¼ c. milk
5 hard cooked eggs, sliced
2 c. (8 oz) shredded cheese
salt + pepper, dash
Eng. muffins, split toasted

Heat oven to 350°. Fry Bacon until crisp,
remove from skillet. Drain fat reserve 2 T.
Saute onion w... Stir in soup,
milk, eggs, chee...

BEQUED B...
5 8 lbs beef bris...
Put meat in large...
Pour ½ bottle of li...
Seal foil tightly -
After 3 hours ad...
Uncover during last
Cut off excess fat the...
SAUCE :
mix over medium heat
½ stick butter
1 cup brown sugar
1 heaping Tbs. d...

Excellent!
Westchester Land cookbook
1 lg. zucchini
1 16 oz. kidney beans
½ c. macaroni - tiny shell
1 T. parsley
Thinly sliced Turkey kilbasa

Minestrone Soup
Dice 5 slices of bacon (½ lb)
1 onion sliced (2)
2 cloves garlic minced
1 jar spaghetti sauce (15 oz)
6 c. water   5 c.
2 beef bouillon cubes
1½ c. each celery & carrots, sliced

Sundried Pasta
saute minced garlic in olive oil
saute
add Broc, saute
ck. Broth, cook down s...
C. ...the sundried tomato...
...ta x...